24 Great Rail-Trails of New Jersey

The Essential Outdoor Guide to

The Garden State's Best Multi-use Recreational Trails

Built on Abandoned Railroad Grades

Craig P. Della Penna

New England Cartographics
Amherst, Massachusetts   1999

Cover design by Bruce Scofield

**Due to changes in conditions, the use of information
in this book is at the sole risk of the user.**

10   9   8   7   6   5   4   3   2   03   02

Publisher's Cataloging-in-publication

Della Penna, Craig.
    24 great rail-trails of New Jersey : the essential outdoor guide
to the Garden State's best multi-use recreational trails built on
abandoned railroad grades / Craig Della Penna.
    212 p.   cm.
    Includes maps and bibliography.
    ISBN 1-889787-04-3
    1. Bicycling.   2. Railroads--History.   3. Bicycle paths--New Jersey.   I. Title.
796.6

Yes Kathleen; life really does begin at 40!!

We welcome any suggestions, comments, or corrections to this book.
Please send them to:
Craig Della Penna
P.O. Box 656, Agawam, MA 01001-0656
or E-mail directly to: railtrail@map.com

Contents

Great Rail-Trails of New Jersey   33

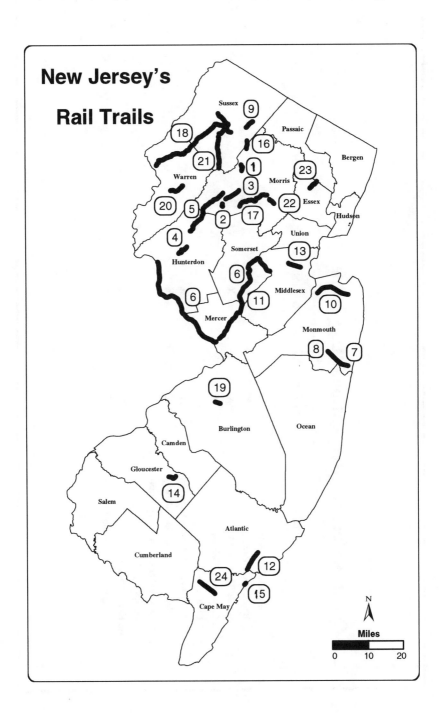

New Jersey's
Rail Trails

Quick Reference Recreational Use Table

*= by permit only

Trail	Hike	Road Bikes	Mt. Bikes	Horses	Wheel Chair	In-Line Skates	X-C Ski
1. Berkshire Valley WMA Trail	X		X	X*			X
2. Black River Park	X		X	X			X
3. Black River WMA	X		X	X*			X
4. Capoolong, Fish and WMA	X		X	X*			X
5. Columbia Trail	X		X	X			X
6. Delaware and Raritan Canal Trail	X	X	X		X	X	X
7. Edgar Felix Memorial Bikeway	X	X	X		X	X	X
8. Freehold and Jamesburg Trail	X		X	X			X
9. Hamburg Mt. WMA	X		X	X*			X
10. Henry Hudson Trail	X	X	X		X		X
11. Kingston Branch Loop Trail	X		X				X

Quick Reference Recreational Use Table

12. Linwood Bikeway	X			X		
13. Middlesex Greenway	X	X		X		X
14. Monroe Township Bikeway	X	X		X	X	X
15. Ocean City Branch	X	X		X	X	
16. Ogden Mine Railroad Path	X		X	X		X
17. Patriot's Path	X		X	X		X
18. Paulinskill Valley Trail	X		X			X
19. Pemberton Rail-Trail	X	X		X	X	X
20. Pequest Fish and WMA	X		X*			X
21. Sussex Branch Railroad Trail	X		X	X		X
22. Traction Line Recreational Trail	X	X			X	X
23. West Essex Trail	X	X		X	X	X
24. Woodbine Railroad Trail	X					X

7

Acknowledgments

The following people had a part in the completion in this book. For their contributions, I am deeply in their debt.

Irv and Isabel Baker, my mentors from Laurel Park in Northampton Massachusetts who always encouraged me. **Bob & Linda Barth** as well as **Len Frank** of the Paulinskill Valley Rail-Trail Committee, an organization of folks with vision and the perseverance to see it through to the end. **Bob Buck** of Warren Massachusetts, whose tales of history on the old New Haven Railroad and the Boston & Albany division of the New York Central inspired me to try to bridge the gap between rail-fans and trail-fans. **David Burwell**, a visionary among mortals whom I am proud to call a friend.

John Cardenas and **Mike Sebastiano** of High Bridge for their contributions to the chapter on the Columbia Trail. **Susan Data-Samtak**, one of New Jersey's many equestrians; I'm thankful for her assistance in making this book a better resource for the members of her community. **Scott & Todd England**, a pair of brothers, one a rail-fan and the other a member of a Rotary Club looking for a good civic project. Putting the two forces together will create the Pemberton Rail-Trail network. **Frank Etzel**, whose hobby of photographing trains has led him to the rail-trails, looking for the Ghost of Industrial Past. **Ronald Dale Karr**, whose classic book *"The Lost Railroads of New England"* was a valuable inspiration. **Larry Lowenthal**, historian for the National Park Service and the author of several books on New Jersey railroads, for letting me pick his brain on some obscure New Jersey railroad facts. **Bill Marsh**, a "big-picture guy" whose talk of bringing more rail-fans into the fold of trail-fans was illuminating and refreshing.

Alan Massey a locomotive engineer whose treks on the trails have helped me immensely. **Larry Miller**, of the NJDEP Office of Natural Lands Management, who provided instrumental assistance and was supportive of this project. **Anne O'Dell** for being such a gracious hostess, editor, teacher of equi-matters, and good friend. **Tom Schmieder** and **Jay McClemmons**, the biking terminators from New Jersey who are rail-fan/trail-fans in the truest sense. **Brian Schmult**, head of New Jersey RailTrails and a fountain of knowledge about New Jersey's abandoned railroads and the right-of-way that they occupied. **Gerry Rice, Walt Stochel, Donald Kahn** and **Bob Takash**, the chief organizers of the Middlesex Greenway that is a unique project taking place in the suburbs of Middlesex County. **Celeste Tracy**, NJDEP Trails Coordinator, who was very supportive of this project. **Chris Ryan** and **Valerie Vaughan** for their vision and patience in the publishing and editing of this book. A special thanks goes to all the trail managers for their assistance with my inquiries.

Foreword
by
Christine Todd Whitman
Governor of New Jersey

As anyone who has spent time in New Jersey knows, there are many ways to enjoy the wonders of nature and the richness of our heritage as the Garden State -- especially, in my case, from the seat of a bicycle.

That's why I am so pleased to see a book like this guide published. To read it -- or better yet, to use it -- is to seize the opportunity to enjoy some of the best assets of the Garden State: our fascinating history, our beautiful landscape, and the rich, diverse mixture of towns along the trails.

New Jersey was a hub of railroad activity a century ago. Today, while we still maintain a network of well-traveled rail lines, many of the state's abandoned lines have been converted to recreational use by our very active hiking and bicycling community.

My hope is that New Jersey can become to the recreational world what it once was to the world of rail transportation. We are working on a plan to preserve, over the next decade, one million more acres of open space and farmland -- approximately half of the available remaining land in the Garden State. Preserving that open space will open up new opportunities for hiking and bicycling, as well as bird-watching, ball-playing, or just soaking up the scenery.

We are also moving forward on a plan I announced in January 1998 to create 2,000 miles of bike paths throughout New Jersey over ten years. These paths will provide countless hours of healthy fun for avid bikers like my family and me, and they have the potential to ease some of the traffic burdens on our crowded roadways. These new paths should add to the enjoyment of those who will read this book and take advantage of the wonderful trails we already have around the state.

As we head into the new millennium, I hope the abandoned rails of the 19th century will remain a permanent legacy of recreation for all who enjoy New Jersey as a perfect place in which to live, work, play, and visit.

Author's Preface

The Day-Job

I am a professional in the railroad industry, the Manager of Railroad Distribution Services (RDS), an intermodal-transloading facility owned by the Pinsly Railroad Company which is headquartered in Westfield, Massachusetts. Pinsly is one of the oldest operators of shortline railroad companies in the country and they currently operate five railroads across the United States. Most of Pinsly's subsidiary railroads include an RDS component to help generate traffic.

At the RDS facility in Massachusetts, we market rail freight into New England by identifying commodities currently traveling across the continent on trucks. By talking with the manufacturers at the point of origin, we find a way to put the cargoes back onto the railroads. If the move is over 750 miles, the rail option is usually cheaper for a shipper of truckload materials. We then route the material via rail to Holyoke, Massachusetts, where a Pinsly property, the Pioneer Valley Railroad, is the final, delivering carrier. We then transload onto short-range trucks and deliver to the final destination, which is usually within 100 miles. The work of taking long-haul trucks off the road ultimately benefits the environment and makes life a little better all around.

The Weekend Archaeologist

In addition to working my day-job, I am also a life-long history buff with an extensive collection of books specializing in railroad history. Living in New England, one cannot escape the constant reminders of the Past. History that you can see and touch is everywhere in New England. This is one of the reasons that we New Englanders like to think of ourselves as the caretakers of the nation's history.

Many times in recent years, my wife and I have gone searching for that history, looking for (apologies to Charles Dickens) the *Ghost of Industrial Past*. We would go exploring for some evidence of railroad infrastructure in the forgotten small towns of New England, seeking out abandoned railroad grades. These old, original lines are not rail-trails, but abandoned Rights-of-Way. (Right-of-Way is an old English term used to describe a path or road that traversed or passed through some adjoining owned lands. I will use the term **RoW** extensively in descriptions of trails or old railroad routes.)

One of my customers at RDS is New England Cartographics, a publisher of outdoor recreation maps and guides that cover the New England region. The owner of NEC, Chris Ryan, was in my office one day in February, 1994, and he noticed my copy of *The Lost Railroads of New England* by R.D. Karr. We started to discuss abandoned railroad rights-of-way and the growing interest in rail-trails, the abandoned railroads which have been converted to multi-use paths. Chris and I discovered that we both were members of the Rails-to-Trails Conservancy, a non-profit organization based in Washington, D.C., that facilitates the conversion of abandonments into linear parks. I had joined the Rails-to-Trails Conservancy in 1990 because I thought their mission statement expressed a great and noble idea: *"The purpose of the Rails-to-Trails Conservancy is to enrich America's communities and countryside by creating a nationwide network of public trails from former rail-lines and connecting corridors.*)

Back in early 1994, there was no definitive guide book on the subject of the rail-trails of New England, so Chris and I decided that such a book might generate some interest. He contracted with me to do the research and write a manuscript. I had no idea of the scope of the project or what I'd find along the way. The goal was to publish a book with all the pertinent information that would make it useful to many different user-groups as well as relevant for the growing awareness of railroad history. I researched and catalogued the trails with an eye to answering some basic questions:

- What were the best trails for families?
- Was there any railroad archaeology still visible?
- What sort of general information might be useful to the public, such as surface, length, permitted uses, and interesting features?

When the *Great Rail-Trails of the Northeast* came out in 1995, it created quite a stir with its coverage of the history of these corridors. Many people discovered that these special corridors were more than just cute paths in the woods. Later, when I saw a number of people on the trails using my book as a reference and guide, I knew that we had stumbled onto something special. In late 1995, Chris Ryan asked me to write more books on the subject, so I went to work on the preparation for a New Jersey rail-trail guide.

Tales from the Trails

Meanwhile, in order to share some of my research and to introduce people to rail-trails, I began in 1996 to present a series of slide lectures that captured some of the rich texture and feelings of serenity that one experiences on these special corridors. Utilizing some of the region's most respected archives, I put together a presentation of images that spanned time at the same location and were shot from the same camera angles.

Tales from the Trails is history seen through the lenses of some of the country's most famous railroad photographers, an experience that bridges the gap between the trail-fans and the rail-fans. I also use the lecture series to help organize and inspire local trail committees in their quest to better their community. I have completed over 130 lectures on this subject and am proud to say that the Rails-to-Trails Conservancy is a supporter of both these efforts and this book. In fact, RTC has brought me on board on a part-time consultant basis as their New England Field Representative.

According to the Rails-to-Trails Conservancy, over $720 million (one-third of the $2.1 billion programmed for Transportation Enhancements spending between 1991 and 1997) has been slated for projects involving historic preservation. This large amount of money has been spent on worthwhile projects all over the country; from restorations of old railroad depots in some communities to providing an inventory of covered bridges in entire states. These funds are only a small part of the growing awareness of history and a growing longing for a way to connect with things as they used to be.

The book you hold in your hands is another contribution to this growth.

The Romance of the Rail-(Trails)

While preparing the research for this book, I noticed something important about rail-trails. The longer a trail had been in place, the more oriented the surrounding community was toward people-scale activities (as opposed to automobile-scale activities), and the more livable it was in terms of spirit. Downtowns had become revitalized and community values were enhanced. These special routes offered the residents a way to reconnect people, neighborhoods, and entire towns in a way that had been almost forgotten.

Revival occurs because the journey on a rail-trail gives the same sense of spiritual or kindred journey that the nation used to experience on the great 'name-trains' of the 1940s, which was probably the last time that large numbers of people were able to connect in this way. Over the past fifty years, towns have been "modernized" -- houses built without porches, developments designed without sidewalks, multi-lane highways providing hours of isolated commuting. Surrounded by public and private spaces that have been stripped of opportunities for human interaction, it's no wonder that people have taken to linear parks and rail-trails in a passionate way. Today, in town after town, the best loved park (where people of all ages meet and get together) is the Rail-Trail. Every day, people who won't or can't speak on the street are greeting one another on Rail-Trails.

A community's rail-trail project of today is a reminder of the same grand vision that created the railroads. Such a vision was well expressed in 1907 by Daniel Burnham, the architect who designed the Union Station in Washington, D.C.

Make no little plans; they have no magic that stirs men's blood and probably themselves will not be realized. Make big plans; aim high in hope and work, remembering that a noble, logical diagram once recorded will never die, but long after we are gone will be a living thing, asserting itself with ever-growing insistence. Remember that our children are going to do things that would stagger us. Let your watch-word be order and your beacon beauty.

The old cliché, the *Romance of the Rails*, is being reincarnated as the *Romance of the Rail-Trails* all over America.

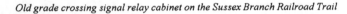

Old grade crossing signal relay cabinet on the Sussex Branch Railroad Trail

THROUGH THE DARKEST HOUR

The railroads are part and parcel of the vital service of supply on which fighting men depend. They know first-hand the darkness of the hour before the dawn. • They follow the progress of the war by the nature and urgency of the burdens they carry—burdens that never lighten through the whole 24 hours of the day. • So through sunshine and shadow, railroad men serve the needs of war. Short on help, short on time, they know the value of every hour and every car. They know that a fighting nation counts on them to deliver the goods that Victory is made of—and doggedly, devotedly, they are sticking to that job. • Some day the dark hour will be behind us. Then our nation will look back on the courage and the will with which we faced it and judge our fiber as a people. • The railroads are working now so that when that day dawns they can, in clear knowledge of a job faithfully discharged, look forward with confidence to finer things to come.

BUY MORE WAR BONDS

ASSOCIATION OF
AMERICAN RAILROADS
ALL UNITED FOR VICTORY

1940s Advertisement, courtesy of TRAINS magazine (Author's collection)

Introduction

Where Did Rail-Trails Come From?

At the beginning of the 20th century, nearly every American city and town had a railroad passing through. Having a railroad was considered a great status symbol, and communities often bid against one another to entice the railroad to come to town. In many cases, palms were greased to facilitate a deal. In the United States, railroads reached a peak in total mileage around World War I, with about 270,000 miles of track. The system has since shrunk to the current total of about 105,000 miles, and much of this loss has occurred during the past few decades. Class 1 mileage diminished from 192,000 miles in 1975 to 108,000 miles in 1995.

In the recently published book *Railroad Mergers: History, Analysis, Insight,* the railroad industry expert Frank Wilner states that mileage may stabilize at no more than 70,000 or 75,000 miles. Wilner believes that, although there will be only one or two mega-railroads running from coast-to-coast, hundreds of shortlines will take over about one half of the difference. Mass-transit and tourist line expansion are expected to expand and Rail-Trails should gather up another 10-to-15,000 miles.

A surprising fact unknown to most people is that the railroads are economically stronger today than in any period since the Second World War. This is true in part because of a law called the Staggers Rail Act of 1980. One component of this law made it easier for railroads to abandon unprofitable branches. In the years prior to Staggers, it was a bureaucratic nightmare for a railroad to abandon lightly used branch lines. Before the Federal government's Interstate Commerce Commission would grant the formal abandonment, the petitioning railroad had to appear at a series of public hearings and present its case to the locals concerned about their loss of a railroad connection.

It was not uncommon for the ICC to deny abandonment because one shipper (who in many cases only had minimal rail traffic) would object to the loss of service. Most times, the whole process took years to complete. Once Staggers was enacted, it took only months to dispose of the unwanted and unprofitable branches. Staggers' streamlined process allowed an additional option; instead of abandonment, a sale to a qualified shortline operator could be considered. Because of their hands-on, local management, these shortlines could solve shipping problems quickly, and customer service became the order of the day.

In the early 1980s, so many branches were being abandoned by railroads and so many of the corridors were being acquired and broken-up by encroaching abutters (adjacent property owners), that Congress passed an amendment to the National Trails System Act in 1983. This one paragraph provision (sometimes called the Humpty Dumpty Wellness Act) instructed the ICC to allow abandoned rail lines to be "railbanked," or set aside for use in the future as a transportation corridor, while being used as a trail in the interim. Without railbanking, many of the abandoned corridors would have disappeared overnight as legal entities, broken into hundreds of small segments that *"not even all the king's horses and all the king's men could put all the pieces together again."*

The controversy surrounding rail-banking resulted in many lawsuits brought by private property owners who objected. Many believed that once railroads were abandoned, the property should revert to the abutters. Ultimately, the United States Supreme Court decided the issue *(Preseault v. United States)* in favor of the recreation community.

In this case, Paul and Patricia Preseault, land developers near Burlington, Vermont, sued over the ex-Rutland right-of-way that ran by their house. The Court ruled that rail banking is constitutional and a legitimate exercise of the power of the Interstate Commerce Commission. However, the case was remanded to a lower court in order to decide if the Preseaults deserved any compensation for the loss of the use of their land. In 1993, Claims Court Judge Christine Nettesheim denied compensation, ruling that the easements were given for railroading purposes, and that "the use to which the easements were put, evolving from railroading to rail banking, is consistent with preserving the easements for rail use." This decision removed the cloud over the nationwide issue of rail banking and spurred the acquisition and development of rail-trails all over the country.

Despite this ruling, in 1997 and 1998, Representative Jim Ryun (R-Kansas) sponsored legislation to either erode or otherwise ruin the rail-banking law. He has failed in all his attempts thus far. Many people remember Jim Ryun from the Olympics during the 1960s as "4 Minute Mile Ryun." The phenomenal runner from years gone by (and a person you would think to be the ultimate linear park advocate) is actually the opponent of the law that facilitates the creation of linear parks for the joggers of today. One of life's small ironies, it only goes to show that in Washington, for any issue, no matter how noble and great, there is an opposing side with lobbyists, supporters, and money.

The *Rails-to-Trails Conservancy* (RTC), formed in 1985 as a Washington, DC-based, non-profit membership and lobbying organization, was set up to educate the public on the benefits of linear parks and to monitor impending abandonment so local or state agencies can act quickly to secure ownership. RTC, with 80,000 members in 1998, has had a hand in the acquisition or improvement of over 1,000 rail-trails across the country, which translates to over 10,000 miles.

Forward-thinking political leaders, such as New Jersey Governor Christie Whitman, recognize the benefits of building more bike facilities rather than more highways. Whitman has recently proposed to have $15 million of the $842 million transportation budget be spent on building 200 miles of bike-ways. Her long-range plan is to build 2,000 miles on such projects. Considering that the state currently has only about 400 miles of such places already in the ground, this proposal would add 50% in the first year and quintuple the original total in ten years. This fairly ambitious goal might not be so far-fetched as an alternative solution to future transportation needs. New Jersey currently has the most heavily used roads and the most cars per square mile than any other state in the nation.

Why Rail-Trails?

The advantage that a railroad has over other modes of land transportation is based on simple principles of physics. A train with steel wheels rides on steel rails which are laid on broad sweeping curves and gentle grades. This is much more fuel-efficient than the number of trucks required to carry the same load over highways. These same principles are what makes a bike trail on an old rail-bed much more efficient and fun to travel. There are few traffic lights, automobiles, sharp turns, or steep climbs (no grades are over 5% in this book). The paved trails are attractive to disabled people in wheel-chairs and parents with strollers. They are also ideal for cross-country skiing and snow-mobiling in winter. In urban areas they provide a bit of recreation space that is appreciated by city folk as well as the businesses that are located "on-line." In some cities, the rail-trails have become a passive commuter highway with people biking or walking to work.

Rural trails provide tourists and dollars, a stimulus to ancillary businesses such as B&Bs and tour groups. On Southwest Virginia's Creeper Trail, a trail over twenty years old, there are competing shuttle companies ferrying trail riders up to the end of the trail, the highest point east of the Mississippi ever served by a railroad. Damascus, one of the communities on the trail, has created twelve bed-and-breakfasts because of the influx of tourists. In fact, Damascus has been designated a *Trail Town USA* because of its friendly attitude towards trail users and the way the community has adopted its trails, including the Appalachian Trail.

In New Freedom Pennsylvania, the Northern Central Railroad and the adjacent Rail-Trail have developed a symbiotic relationship, being side-by-side in the same corridor for some twenty miles. It is a good example of the can-do attitude that permeates the modern shortline railroad industry and a prime example of Trail-with-Rail, shared corridors. Ken Bitten, the General Manager of the Northern Central Railroad, has instituted an interesting marketing program whereby trail users (and their bikes) are shuttled from one end to the other. You can ride your bike and tour the beautiful central Pennsylvania countryside to the end of the trail and then take the train back to the point of origin.

Some of the rural trails also provide a unique perspective on the local wildlife. Bob Spoerl, of the State of New Hampshire's Department of Resources and Economic Development, pointed out one feature that makes rail-trails special. Whenever there is a pond or other body of water bisected by the trail, the wildlife found there would be normally inaccessible, being in the middle of the pond, but from the trail it can be viewed up-close.

Viewing the RoW on a Rail-Trail is different now from how the riders of yesteryear's passenger train viewed it. They could see only to the left or the right. In those days, the only people who could see the RoW in a straight-ahead format were the civil engineer who designed the cuts and fills of the RoW and the operating engineer who ran the train. With the conversion of the RoW into a Rail-Trail, the users of today can connect with the lay-of-the-land in a way that is unlike any other experience encountered in normal day-to-day experience.

One of the civil engineers who deserves mention is U.S. Army Lieutenant George Whistler, the father of some of the earliest railroads in the U.S. He built a line through the Berkshire Hills of Western Massachusetts for the Western Railroad which opened in 1841 and was a marvel of the time. In fact, it is still in operation as the Conrail-CSX mainline into New England. It sees thirty trains every day and runs over two mortar-less stone arch bridges built in 1840. Ironically, Whistler's wife became more famous than he did when she was immortalized in a painting done by their son. The painting, of course, was called *Whistler's Mother*.

Historical tidbits like this can be found everywhere along the rail-trails. People are generally surprised to find interesting old places and buildings right there under their noses, just waiting to be rediscovered. Support for the historic preservation effort in this country is being enhanced by the growth of rail-trails. In Pemberton, New Jersey, for example, the Rotary Club is sponsoring a Rail-Trail project as their big community enhancement project for 1998-99 (See Ride # 19). Such an endeavor will strengthen their community and lead to a renaissance of the spirit.

Lonely depots and stations, some with semaphore signals that no longer communicate with trains, are metaphors for a language no longer spoken. Some of these buildings are being restored to their former grandeur; not to provide shelter while awaiting transport to another place, but instead to provide a gateway to another time. Sampling the trails within this book can mean more than just walking or biking in solitude. You also have the chance to connect with the path of the country's optimism and vibrancy.

"The railroad runs right through my store!"

"*WHAT I MEAN IS THIS: the railroad connects my store . . . and my business . . . with every other town and city in the whole country.*

"*That means I can give my customers the same kind of merchandise—the same up-to-the-minute goods — that folks in the big towns enjoy.*

"*So you see why I figure that the railroad is really in partnership with me, and with every other local merchant.*"

•

Yes, throughout their exciting history, America's railroads have played a big part in helping to develop community life and business.

The railroads are *local* business. They employ people wherever they run. They buy supplies in seven out of every eight counties of the U. S.

They own property in every community they serve—and pay local taxes. In fact, as much as half the tax money received by many counties is paid by the railroads. And that can't be said of any other form of commercial transportation!

American railroads are working to improve still further their essential service to the nation's people, to expand their partnership with the nation's business. The vast amount of new equipment required will be bought with railroad money, without federal, state, or municipal aid. For the railroads, like other local business, are self-supporting—neither asking nor expecting financial aid from other taxpayers. Safe, dependable, inexpensive—the railroads continue to be the backbone of America's transportation service.

1940s Advertisement, courtesy of TRAINS magazine (Author's collection)

The Long-Time-A-Comin' Trail

The Story of Paulinskill Valley Trail (Ride # 18)

By Bill Weiler

How long does it take for an abandoned railroad bed to become a state park? Easy, you say? Read and learn how long it can take and how difficult and drawn out the task proved to be.

The right-of-way was a natural for a trail. It extended from near Columbia, on the Delaware, through Blairstown, and followed the Paulinskill to within three miles of Newton and ended in Sparta Junction in Sussex County. Its total length is twenty-seven miles. It passed through farmlands, woods and small hamlets.

The New Jersey Department of Environmental Protection (DEP) held a public meeting in Blairstown on June 13, 1985, to announce their intention to purchase the site. What a commotion that caused! Local community members came out in droves. The most vocal ones were anti-trail and were mad as hornets. There were a fair number of pro-trail people present, but we were not prepared for anything like the storm we encountered. Such stern opposition set us all, including the DEP, back on our heels. Landowners with property adjacent to the trail had organized, calling themselves the "Railroad Right of Way Repurchase Association." They also had the backing of many other local landowners, some of them long-time citizens of Warren County. They also seemed to have the support of just about every local politician, including the state senator, two state assemblymen, the three freeholders from Warren County, and all the politicians from the bordering towns -- mayors, councilmen, and planning board members.

Our task, obviously, was to prove that strong local backing, especially political backing, did exist in the trail's home district. Under Len Frank's leadership, an ad hoc committee began meeting at the Frank's residence. Len had been a long-time leader in the local Sierra Club chapter and was well qualified to coordinate this effort. Wondering what we could do, we decided our first step would be to lead hikes on the trail. We maintained booths at the county fairs in Sussex and Warren and at the Sussex Air show. Roberta Bramhall made up large displays with huge maps of the trail accented by many photographs.

We became organized as the Paulinskill Valley Trail Committee, soliciting memberships at $10 a year and with this money, printed a pamphlet to help promote our cause. Our progress was still painfully slow. Several elections went by, but produced no political backing for our trail. We had been naive enough to believe that perhaps the elections would produce a surprise but they never did.

Then came a break. In the summer of 1986, the Sussex Voice issued a reader's poll on the trail. The Voice was a new monthly magazine, and although we had no way of knowing it, their poll eventually would help lead us to victory. The poll was printed, and came out just in time for the Sussex Fair in August 1986. The poll consisted of nine questions. Copies were printed out and used at our booth and the Voice booth at the fair. We promoted the poll vigorously and as a result we got 650 responses of which 90.6% were in favor of the trail. A second reader's poll in 1987 gave us 968 responses with 92.5% in favor. In 1988, the Voice advised us that they would not repeat the poll for a third year. We made hasty arrangements to publish our own poll under the sponsorship of the County Federation of Sportsmen's Clubs. This resulted in 614 responses with 97% in favor of the trail.

Public backing for the trail had been amply demonstrated, but the politicians looked the other way. We wrote to some and contacted a few more, but without results. We began to think that all our work was for nothing. Little did we know that someone was out there watching all of this and was ready to do something about it.

Wally Wirths of Wantage in Sussex County contacted the Sussex Freeholders, Joseph Del Bagno, Victor Marotta and Michael LaRose, and told them about the trail and the results of the polls. They paid attention. Freeholder LaRose hiked along a portion of the trail and promptly reported to them that it was a "hidden gem" and must be saved. The three freeholders promptly drew up and signed a resolution that the state should buy the trail. This was the political support that Governor Kean needed to see, and shortly thereafter he authorized the DEP to purchase the trail.

For more on this trail, see Ride # 18, The Paulinskill Valley Trail.

Each generation has its rendezvous with the land, for despite our fee titles and claims of ownership, we are all but brief tenants on this planet. By choice or default, we carve out a land legacy for our heirs.

Stewart Udall, former Secretary of the Interior

How to Use This Book

Each Rail-Trail description in this guide is set up like the example below:

17 Patriots' Path *(Ride # and the official name of the trail)*
Rockaway Valley Railroad
(The most commonly known former railroad owner/operator)

Endpoints: Speedwell Park to Sunrise Lake
(These are the normally accepted endpoints which make for a safe trip. They may not represent the entire abandoned railroad branch, but they are the safe or approved sections.)

Location: Morris County, Township of Morris
(The county/counties where the trail is located, along with the cities, towns, townships or boroughs that it passes through.)

Length: 5.1 miles
*(This is the length of the trail **one way**, measured on a bike odometer. This length may differ from that listed in other sources or printed matter.)*

Surface: Asphalt, ballast cinder gravel, and sand
(The materials used to make the trail surface.) These may include:

   Gravel; which is coarse sand that drains well and locks together to provide a firm surface;

   Sand; loose beach sand that tends to be soft and can swallow up tires;

   Cinder; the coal by-product left over after burning. Gray to dark gray in color, this was used by the railroads years ago because of its unlimited availability and its unique ability to prevent the growth of weeds. This is a good firm surface.

   Ballast; Large angular stones, usually about 2 or 3 inches in diameter, on which the original track structure was placed. This type of surface is not much fun to ride a bike on.

Map(s): Morristown and Mendham in the U.S.G.S. 1:24,000 series and Newark in the 1:100,000 series.
(The most current United States Geologic Survey Topographic maps which show the trail. If more than one is in use because of over-lap, the starting map is listed first, followed by others in order of trail direction. The ones normally used are from the 1:24,000 series, where one inch equals 2,000 feet or 0.4 mile. In some cases, the name of the corresponding 1:100,000 series map is also listed. The maps in this book are compiled from the Map-Tech CD ROMs of the Topo Scout® series for New Jersey.)

Uses: All non-motorized uses
(The different uses that are approved for the trail. See Tables, pages 6-7.)

To get there: *(The directions to get to the best place to start the trail.)*

Contact: **Morris County Park Commission**
                   P.O. Box 1295
                   Morristown, NJ 07962-1295
                   973-326-7600

(This is the person or agency who can be contacted to provide information and local color. Sometimes it is an official government manager or it may be a resident that has volunteered to accept calls, even at their home. Either way, this is the best person to write or call about the trail.)

Local Bed & Breakfast: *(Some of the nearest B&Bs or other lodging nearest to the trail-head. There is no rating as to their quality of service).*

Local Resources for bike repairs:

(The bike shops listed here are a partial listing of the ones that were near the trail and willing to be included in the book at the time of publication. It should be noted that this type of business is prone to being seasonal or having a high turnover, so be alert for changes.)

Following the listings (as in the example given above) is the main body of the trail history. The information presented is not meant to be the last word on that trail's former owners. It will, however, give an idea of why it was there and sometimes the reason for its abandonment.

The odometer-based mileage guide comes next. This will indicate important geological and man-made features along the route. Having an odometer on your bike is not required, but it will increase your enjoyment of the trail and will prevent your missing some of the small pieces of railroad archaeology that are mentioned. The least expensive bicycle odometer can be bought for about $20.00.

Out-and-Back versus Car Spotting

The description and length of each bike trail in this guide is for *one way* only. It is assumed that you will park your car at the beginning of the trail and ride "out and back." The author, who is not by any stretch of the imagination a bike pro, was able to ride every trail in this book out and back. You may prefer, however, to spot cars (parking one at each end of the trail). It is your choice. **Just remember to double the mileage if you are riding out and back.**

Bicycling Equipment and Safety

The following information will allow you to make many enjoyable trips on *The 24 Great Rail-Trails of New Jersey*. Proper equipment and safety practices can make the difference between a pleasant experience and a disappointing one. To ride the non-asphalt trails in this book, you will need at least a Hybrid Bike. Such bikes are relatively new on the market and are best recognized by their "fat" tires. The width of the tires prevents the bike from sinking into the sand or dirt found on some of the trails. Another common feature of these bikes is the greater number of gears compared to the old 10-speeds. This feature is welcome when you need an extremely low gear to go through sand or other soft surfaces. The very low gears also will allow you to climb steep gradients with less difficulty.

A cyclo-computer-odometer will make riding the *Great Rail-Trails of the New Jersey* more enjoyable. Electronic odometers cost as low as $20.00 and are a valuable addition to any bike. Do not use a mechanical type as they are prone to failure and are not very accurate. The electronic types have a trip-odometer that can be re-set, plus clock and mile-per-hour functions. More expensive models indicate cadence, elapsed time, pulse rate monitor, kilometers, etc. The sky's the limit. You must, however, set them properly to match your tire size. Slight variations may introduce different odometer readings than those indicated in the trail descriptions.

Your bike should also have a rack to hold panniers or other type of packs. Rain-gear should be one of the first items into the pack. A handle-bar pack is a useful addition to hold maps (or this guide) and other readily needed materials. A water bottle that mounts on the frame of the bike is a necessity.

To get to the trails means that you will probably be transporting the bike with your car. Do not waste money on a cheap, unknown brand of bike rack. The best money you can spend will be on the highest quality rack you can obtain for your specific vehicle. Do not skimp here. You do not want to be losing your bike off the roof or trunk while on the highway.

The foremost concern while on a bicycle should be safety. When arriving at any trail-head you should first look for any signage that has to do with safety on that trail. Sometimes there is a different way of doing things on that trail that may be new to you or others in your party. Here are a few rules that apply to all rail-trails.

Guidelines for Bicycle Safety

(1) Wear a helmet. Broken bones and torn muscles will heal but a broken head will not.

(2) Wear bright colors. This is particularly important where vehicles may be encountered. Plan to be seen.

(3) Make sure your bike is in proper working order, especially the brakes.

(4) Invest in a rearview mirror, either the type that mounts on the handlebar or the kind that mounts on the helmet.

(5) Ride on the right side of the trail, and sound a bell or call out when passing.

(6) Ride responsibly with confidence and within your capabilities. Do not ride beyond your endurance, and if you ride alone, let someone know your itinerary.

(7) Carry a small tool kit and know how to use it to do minor, on-site repairs, including spare tube for fixing a flat tire.

Restored antique cast iron grade crossing sign on the D & R Canal Trail

Something New

ON THE TABLE!

For the first time a way has been found to put into a locomotive the same kind of power that sends big battleships forward—*turbine drive!*

Developed by Pennsylvania Railroad research in conjunction with engineering staffs of Westinghouse Electric Corporation and the Baldwin Locomotive Works, this new kind of locomotive power adds extra smoothness in fast runs—and many other notable advantages.

No bigger than your electric refrigerator, the steam turbine itself can produce power to pull the heaviest loads at high speeds. And the engineman controls the whole operation with a single small lever which works like a gear-shift on an automobile!

One of the most important changes in the power principle of the steam locomotive in over 100 years, the turbine drive engine gives promise of a great future in the field of train transportation.

PENNSYLVANIA RAILROAD
Serving the Nation

1940s Advertisement, courtesy of TRAINS magazine (Author's collection)

Morris County's Adopt-A-Trail Program

The Morris County Park Commission has recently started an Adopt-A-Trail Program, which is a unique way for citizens and organizations to positively affect the environment while providing a valuable volunteer service to the community. Adopters maintain (and in some cases plan and build) a trail or portions of a trail, greatly assisting the Park Commission to meet its goal of providing safe and attractive trails and park facilities. Adopters may consist of individuals, families, or groups and organizations, e.g. clubs, camps, scouts, etc. Everyone is welcome to sign up, regardless of experience. Basic and advanced training in trail maintenance is provided by the Morris County Park Commission.

Adopting a trail provides you with an opportunity to commune with nature, stay physically fit, and attain a personal sense of accomplishment and pride. You will receive the Adopt-A-Trail newsletter and be invited to a special volunteer recognition event. Most importantly, volunteer efforts help the Morris County Park Commission keep many miles of trails available to the public.

Adopters perform basic maintenance on a trail or section of trail. The basic tasks are cutting brush, cleaning out existing drainage, painting blazes, and picking up litter. With further training, experience, and approval from the Park Commission, adopters may perform more complicated jobs such as construction of waterbars, rock steps, or bridges. In some cases, a volunteer may design and/or build a trail from scratch.

All interest and experience levels are welcome; the tools and equipment are provided for adopters. Adopters may work on their own schedule and pace. A minimum of three trips per year are needed to maintain most trails. You will be asked to file trail reports three times a year. The best times are generally during the spring thaw to correct winter blowdowns and plugged drainage, the early summer to cut back overgrown sections, and the fall to repair the trail after a season of heavy use. Adopters can request the assistance of the Park Commission, and are welcome to involve family, friends, and other groups in trail work.

If you would like to adopt a section of a trail in one of the Morris County Parks call the Trails Coordinator for the Morris County Park Commission at (973) 326-7604

The Green Acres Program of New Jersey

Imagine a New Jersey where ....

- protected greenways criss-cross the state, connecting parks and neighborhoods, safeguarding streams and water supplies, and providing opportunities for walking, jogging, biking, and other recreation;
- abundant parks and recreation areas enhance the urban, suburban, and rural areas;
- entire landscapes are left forever wild to protect New Jersey's rich diversity of plants and animals;
- areas for scenic beauty and historic significance are preserved for public enjoyment;
- beautiful urban parks and waterfront promenades provide relief from the pressures of urban life and help revitalize the social and economic fabric of New Jersey;
- state agencies work in partnership with county and municipal governments, nonprofit conservation groups, and private land owners to preserve the state's dwindling open spaces.

The Green Acres Program of New Jersey is working to transform these images into reality. Created in 1961 to meet the state's growing needs for recreation and conservation, Green Acres is committed to preserving New Jersey's rich natural, historic and cultural heritage. As of 1998, voters have overwhelmingly approved nine bond issues, earmarking over $1.4 billion for land acquisition and park development. Hundreds of public parks have been developed and nearly 400,000 acres of conservation and recreation land have been or are being preserved with Green Acres funds.

Preserving Open Space

Green Acres focuses primarily on acquiring land that creates linkages between existing protected land in order to form open space corridors. These corridors provide linear habitats for wildlife to move through, parkland for recreation, and areas of scenic beauty which lie between towns and urban centers. Green Acres gathers other public and private partners together to assist in buying and managing open space. The Program works with municipal and county governments, nonprofit organizations, and the state Farmland Preservation Program to meet compatible conservation goals. The cooperative projects succeed because the preservation of large tracts of land is easier when costs are shared. Green Acres also accepts donations of conservation and recreation land to the State. Since the 1980s, over 5,400 acres of land have been donated by private citizens interested in land preservation.

Restful relaxation in luxurious surroundings . . . every mile will be a memorable moment in the new, exquisitely appointed Observation-Lounge.

Take it Easy when you travel...

Whether it's a vacation or business trip, a pleasant interlude of real rest and relaxation begins the moment you step aboard a C & E I train. You just relax and take it easy as the miles glide by.

When you get hungry, visit the dining car and you'll find tempting foods and friendly hospitality awaiting you . . . foods expertly pre-pared by chefs who take a genuine pride in "setting a good table."

Soon, C & E I's new CHICAGO-LINERS will be ready to go into service . . . bringing you the very finest in luxurious, high-speed transportation. So when you travel, just specify C & E I . . . you'll get there swiftly, quietly and safely while you "take it easy."

New diner with diagonal seating will offer the ultimate in roomy comfort . . . in an inviting atmosphere of gracious dining.

New day coaches with reclining chairs of advanced design for extra leg room . . . lounging freedom . . . smoother riding comfort.

Reproductions Courtesy Pullman-Standard

CHICAGO & EASTERN ILLINOIS railroad
The Chicago Line

1950 Advertisement, courtesy of TRAINS magazine (Author's collection)

Funding Recreation Facilities

Recreation needs are as diverse as the people who play. To meet these needs, Green Acres funds a multitude of parks in a variety of settings providing recreation that spans the seasons: swimming beaches, basketball courts, trails along wooded streams, pristine natural areas brimming with wildlife, and city playgrounds brimming with children. These parks and open spaces boast the Green Acres sign, showing the public how their investment is being spent. Located in rural, suburban, and urban areas, parks play an important role in sustaining New Jersey's high quality of life. To learn more about this program, call 609-984-0500 or write to Green Acres Program, P.O. Box 412, Trenton, NJ 08625-0412.

Future Trails in New Jersey

Trail	Length	County
Cross Jersey Trail	*15*	*Morris; Hunterdon*
Newfield Branch	*20*	*Atlantic*
Garfield to Passaic	*1.8*	*Bergen; Passaic*
Gloucester County Trails Project	*21*	*Gloucester*
Henry Hudson Trail Extension	*1.7*	*Monmouth*
Bikepath Extension	*3.3*	*Atlantic*
Medford to Mt. Holly	*5.75*	*Burlington*
Middle Township Bikeway	*0.5*	*Cape May*
Monmouth Heritage Trail	*12*	*Monmouth*
West Morris Greenway	*24*	*Morris*

To learn more about these exciting future projects, call the county parks or local planning departments.

East Coast Greenway

A multi-use and urban parallel to the Appalachian Trail, the **East Coast Greenway** is a 2,000-mile-long, shared use trail network being developed to link cities, suburbs and towns from Maine to Florida. By connecting existing trails with new segments, a continuous, mostly traffic-free path is being created to serve walkers, cyclists, skaters, equestrians, skiers, and wheelchair users. This safe and green route will provide a place for exercise, recreation, and social interchange. It will also function as a local transportation facility, encouraging people to leave their cars in the garage in favor of a healthier walk or bicycle trip to the store, school, or work. As a long distance route, it will attract large numbers of Americans and foreign tourists to whom adventure travel on bike or foot is an appealing way to explore the historically and naturally rich East Coast region.

One section of the East Coast Greenway which is currently open for use in New Jersey is the D & R Canal State Park, the leg from Princeton to East Brunswick, a small part of which is the **Kingston Branch Loop Trail** *(Ride # 11 in this book).*

The East Coast Greenway Alliance

The **East Coast Greenway Alliance**, founded in 1991, is a national, non-profit membership organization dedicated to making this greenway a reality. Working through state committees, the Alliance is partnering with local citizens, national, state and local organizations and agencies. The chief goals are to identify the route, advance new trails to close the gaps, dedicate and sign completed portions, and develop user information. The Alliance will encourage travel services such as B&Bs, hostels, food and bike shops, and work to ensure a high quality of maintenance to enable the public to travel the route easily and in comfort.

For information about joining, contact:
Karen Votava, Executive Director, **East Coast Greenway Alliance**
135 Main Street Wakefield, RI 02879   401-789-1706
Email: ecga @ juno.com   Web site: *www.greenway.org*

The "Big Four" in rail-trail development in Middlesex County
(Left to right: Gerry Rice, Bob Takash, Walt Stochel, & Brian Schmult, head of NJ Rail Trails)

Public timetable for the L & NE Railroad, circa 1913 (Author's collection)

The Great Rail-Trails of New Jersey

Rail-Trails are a unique experience. They start in your town instead of a long drive away, but quickly take you through extremely varied scenery: residential areas, forests, industrial regions, mountain sides, wetlands, and swamps. They connect communities to each other and to other parks.

Since the turn of the century, over 800 miles of railroad corridor has been abandoned within New Jersey alone. Much of this is still intact, and a small portion has been preserved and added to the state's trail system. If you enjoy the trails listed here, and would like to have more, please consider putting some time into preservation activity.

New Jersey RailTrails (NJRT) is a non-profit, volunteer, conservation corporation that encourages rail-trail creation in New Jersey. Contact NJRT at P.O. Box 23, Pluckemin, NJ 07978. (215) 340-9974.

-- From the brochure about NJRT by Brian Schmult.

Multi-use action along the Paulinskill Valley Trail (photo by Susan Data-Samtak)

The Great Rail-Trails
of New Jersey

Sussex Branch Railroad Trail crosses underneath the abandoned Lackawanna Cutoff via tunnel. Note the derelict telegraph pole with numerous insulators.

1 Berkshire Valley WMA Trail

Edison Branch of the Central Railroad of New Jersey (CNJ)

Endpoints: Gordon Road to Minnisink Road in Roxbury Township
Location: Morris County, Roxbury Township
Length: 2.1 miles
Surface: Cinder
Map(s): Dover, U.S.G.S. 1:24,000 series
Uses: All non-motorized uses. Horses by permit only.

To get there: From just north of I-80, take Route 15 west to Berkshire
Valley Road and follow this for 2.3 miles. Follow this to Gordon Road
where you will take a right, and then go 0.3 miles. Just past the intersection
of Country Road, you will see the start of the trail on the right. About 20
feet further on is a small access road, surfaced with white stone and leading
to a small parking lot which is the only approved place to park.

Contact:
John Piccolo
Black River Wildlife Management Area
275 North Road, Chester, NJ 07930
908-879-6252

Local Bed & Breakfast: The Publick House, 111 W. Main St., Chester NJ
07930   (908) 879-6878

Local resources for bike repair/rentals:
Route 15 Bicycle Outlet, Route 15, Lake Hopatcong, NJ 973-663-1935

The historical importance of this trail has been well described by Larry
Lowenthal, the author of *Iron Mine Railroads of Northern New Jersey*. "All
of the Iron Mine railroads were small; some were classic short lines. They
were all quaint and several had truly unique features. Yet, of them all, the
Ogden Mine Railroad comes closest to being a legend."

What, you didn't realize that New Jersey had iron mines? In the highlands
north of I-80 and west of I-287, the whole area was once pock-marked with
iron and other mineral mines. Copper and zinc were some of the more
common ones, while one of the rare minerals was Franklinium. The only
place on earth this is found is in Franklin, New Jersey.

Some of the iron mines of this part of New Jersey date back to earlier than the American Revolution, when the ore was transported out to the furnaces by oxen. Later, water borne connections were afforded to the Morris Canal by way of Lake Hopatcong. A railroad connection to the mining industry in this area was not conceived until the Civil War period. In 1864, the Ogden Mine Railroad was chartered by a group of men who were mainly from eastern Pennsylvania. The line was finished in 1866 and ran only from the mines north of Lake Hopatcong at Edison to Nolan's Point on the eastern shore of the Lake where the transfer to the canal barge was made.

The Central Railroad of New Jersey did not complete the Lake Hopatcong Railroad until 1882. It ran from the Lake at Nolan's Point to their main E-W route just south of today's I-80. The Ogden Mine line north of Nolan's Point was acquired in 1887. The entire branch from the mainline to the Ogden Mine was 15.2 miles. The *Odgen Mine Railroad Path* (Ride # 16), is actually the continuation of this *Berkshire Valley* trail, and begins about five miles further north of this trail.) Here on the southern reaches of the branch, there was one notable feature that became the signature of the line. At Nolan's Point, the resort Hotel Breslin was the destination of over 50,000 visitors every summer. This was one of the huge old-style grand hotels that featured the typical verandahs of the day, as well as over 400 hundred rooms; each with a view. This hotel was in operation from the late 1880s to the late 1920s when the automobile began to make an impression on tourism traffic. The end of scheduled passenger service took place in 1928, and only a few "fan-train" trips tip-toed up the branch in the 1930s. The freight traffic slowly dried up as the iron mines were played out and the general traffic was not enough to support the line.

Most of this "other traffic" was ice. Cut from the Lake and stored in well insulated buildings for the coming summer, this commodity was a staple on many railroads in the days before refrigeration. The CNJ formally abandoned the upper end in 1935, while the lower half lasted until 1941. Today you cannot bike as far as Nolan's Point because the RoW was sold off to developers long ago and the sections near the Lake are nowhere to be seen. The general description of the terrain along this trail is called pitched, due to the many ravines and hills. The one major mad-made feature is a pipeline which runs along the trail's Row for half the length of the trail.

0.0 miles: The trail is gated with an orange PVC pipe that is seen on other New Jersey trails. Some cinder in the beginning as you head into the hardwood forest while going past one house.
0.4 miles: On a bit of a cinder fill and the trail will be bending to the right.
0.6 miles: Continuing to go uphill as the vista of the surrounding valley opens ahead of you and on the right.

1. Berkshire Valley WMA Trail

Scale: 1" = 0.8 mile
Travel South to North

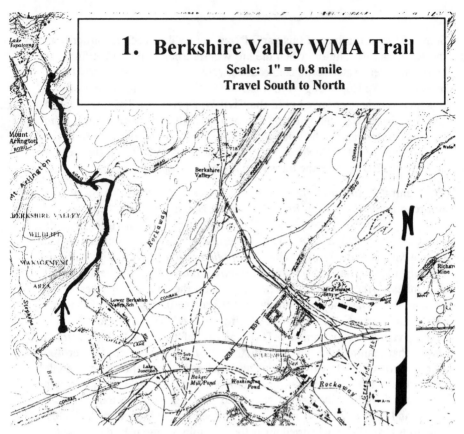

0.7 miles: A pipeline now appears and takes up residence on the RoW with you. This is made of steel and is about 30" in diameter.

1.2 miles: Still heading uphill and now into a cut where the pipeline heads underground.

1.4 miles: On a bit of a fill about 12 feet tall, the trail curves to the right.

1.7 miles: Sharp drop-off to the right as you are on another fill.

1.9 miles: In the spring or other wet times of the year, a stream will be coursing down the RoW in this area.

2.1 miles: The trail diverges here. The right fork is the original RoW into a cut and can be very wet at times. The dirt bikes have worn in a new path to the left and up above. The trail ends ahead at a town garage and storage yard. This is the end of the trail at Minnisink Road.

The Jefferson Township Public Health Center is part of the complex here. This area was originally the location of the station at Minnisink Road and the site of the branch's worse train wreck. Here in 1900, a mixed train (one that had both passenger cars and freight cars) was hit by an ice train, but with only four minor injuries, it was not a major event.

2 Black River Park

Hacklebarney Branch of the Central New Jersey Railroad

Endpoints: Chester (all within the County Park)
Location: Morris County, Chester Township
Length: 1.1 miles
Surface: Gravel and dirt
Map(s): Chester, U.S.G.S. 1:24,000 series
Uses: All non-motorized uses.

To get there: Take Route 206 to Chester, then travel West on Route 24 for approximately 2 miles until you reach Morris County Park Commission's Cooper Mill on the left. Park in the lot adjacent to the mill complex.

Contact:
Morris County Park Commission
P.O. Box 1295, Morristown, NJ 07962-1295
973-326-7600

Local Bed & Breakfast: The Publick House, 111 W. Main Street, Chester, NJ 07930   (908) 879-6878

Local resources for bike repair:
Route 15 Bicycle Outlet, Route 15, Lake Hopatcong NJ.   973-663-1935
Nelson's Cycle Shop, Hwy. 24, Chester, NJ 07930   908-879-7677

The following information is from a brochure put out by the New Jersey RailTrails, a state-wide non-profit group that works to turn abandoned railroads into multi-use public trails. Information about joining is available by to P.O. Box 23, Pluckemin, NJ 07978, or by calling 215-249-3669.

The discovery of iron ore brought prosperity to Chester, and it also brought railroads. Among them was the Hacklebarney branch of the High Bridge Railroad., which later became part of the Central Railroad of New Jersey (CNJ). Just 3.5 miles long., this branch line was built in 1883 to serve the iron mines along the Black River. In use for less than 30 years, the branch enabled the Hacklebarney and Langdon mines to transport their ore northward to the Chester Furnace and the Chester branch of the CNJ. At the Hacklebarney mines, ore cars were loaded directly using a large loading trestle, and the mines also boasted a "Roaster," a furnace which was used to reduce the sulfur content of the ore.

Although iron mines had existed in the Hacklebarney area as early as 1760, it was not until their peak in the 1880s that they became truly productive. In this prosperous period, the mines shipped as much as 31,000 tons of ore annually, and in one winter's day of 1894 the branch shipped 500 tons of ice which had been cut from Hacklebarney Pond. But Chester's prosperity was not to last. In the 1890s, vast deposits of ore which were less expensive to mine were discovered in Minnesota, and the line was quickly abandoned. In 1900, local schoolchildren were dismissed from their classes early so they could watch the last train run along the branch, removing the tracks and ties as it went.

Today the remnants of the branch lie within New Jersey Wildlife Management lands to the North of Route 24, and within Morris County Park Commission property to the south. Although the northern section can be hiked, it is overgrown and almost impassable in some places. The southern section below Route 24 is suitable for hiking and biking, and the trail is a poignant reminder of the once industrial nature of what has now become a beautiful, unspoiled river valley.

0.0 miles: After parking at the Cooper Mill lot, follow the paved path towards the old mill. Use the stairs at the south side of the mill to reach a small path which continues towards the river. Just downstream you will see a raised embankment where the rail branch one spanned the river. Cross over the mill's tail-race nearer the river and climb up the embankment.
0.1 miles: Once on top of the embankment, look to the other side of the river where you will see the northern section of the trail bed, much of which has been eliminated for the expansion of Route 24. Proceed southward in a generally downstream direction, along the rail bed.
0.3 miles: After passing through a curving cut, you will come upon a low stone bridge which provides drainage for the area on the left. Note that the stones on this simple bridge use a post and lintel construction to create a pair of water outlets.
0.4 miles: To the right is the northern section of Hacklebarney Pond, created by a dam to provide water power for the forge and machine shops below.
0.5 miles: Up the hill to the east are remnants of the once plentiful iron mines in Chester. Rock waste from the mining operation are clearly visible. Here, one can still find small pieces of magnetite with a compass. The compass needle will swing noticeably when an ore sample is nearby.
0.6 miles: Still traveling southward on the rail bed, you will encounter a chain link fence to the left which encloses some of the Hacklebarney mines. During peak operation, there were mines on both sides of the river here. This section of the trail marks what was once the busiest section of the rail branch.

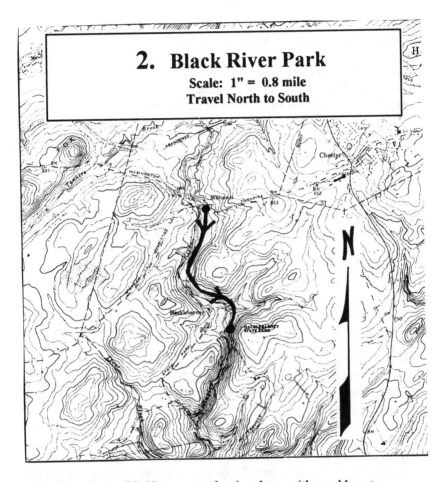

2. Black River Park

Scale: 1" = 0.8 mile
Travel North to South

0.7 miles: A small bridge crosses the river here, with an old, water-powered mill still standing below. Although the rail bed becomes less distinct, continue traveling south on the same side of the river.

1.1 miles: The rail branch once crossed the river here as it continued in a southwesterly direction for another mile to serve the Langdon mine and other small workings. This point marks the end of the railroad-related section of the trail, as the remaining rail bed has either been incorporated into roadways or lies on private property. However, for those who wish to continue their hike/bike, a trail continues along the river, still within Morris County Park Commission property.

3 Black River WMA Trail

Chester Branch of the Lackawanna Railroad (DL&W)

Endpoints: Chestnut Hill Road to nearly Ironia Road, Chester
Location: Morris County, Chester Township
Length: 4.0 miles
Surface: Gravel and dirt
Map(s): Chester, U.S.G.S. 1: 24,000 series
Uses: All non-motorized uses. Horses by permit only.

To get there: Take Route 206 to County Road 513 to Main Street to a left or west onto Oakdale Road. Go approximately 0.2 mile and then right onto Pleasant Hill Road. The trail-head is on the left after the driveway of the Hermits of Bethlehem. An orange marker is across the trail to the right.

Contact:
John Piccolo, Black River Wildlife Management Area
275 North Road, Chester, NJ 07930 908-879-6252

Local Bed & Breakfast: The Publick House, 111 W. Main St.,
Chester NJ 07930 (908) 879-6878

Local resources for bike repair/rentals:
Route 15 Bicycle Outlet, Route 15, Lake Hopatcong, (973) 663-1935
Nelson's Cycle Shop, Hwy. 24, Chester, NJ 07930 (908) 879-7677

This trail is located on the original grade of the Chester Branch of the Delaware Lackawanna & Western Railroad. This branch ran ten miles from a mainline junction just west of Dover and Wharton to Chester. The rail-trail is on the last 4.5 miles, between Ironia Road and the site of the old Chester Depot (now Simmonds Precision) on Oakdale Road. The Chester Branch was built in 1868 to serve the needs of the local iron mining industry, whose boom lasted into the 1890s. In 1873, a competing rail line was built to serve the area from Long Valley. Between it and the Chester Branch terminus was the Chester Furnace complex (just east of Route 206 between Furnace Road and the Black River). The Chester Branch carried many train loads of iron ore from the area mines, along with ingots from the Chester Furnace, to the furnaces and foundries in Wharton and Dover. The 1892 discovery of easily accessible, higher grade ore in the Mesabi Range of Minnesota ended the local boom. Passenger service began in early 1933 and the track was removed from Succasunna to Chester later that year. In 1965, the section from Ironia to Chester came into state ownership and is now part of the Black River Wildlife Management Area.

The trail is suitable for all off-road non-motorized uses. It is not improved, but has a hard cinder base. Horses require an annual permit to use Wildlife Management Areas. Contact Fish, Game & Wildlife at (609) 984-6211 for information. Note that the area is managed for hunting and fishing, so take appropriate precautions during hunting season.

0.0 miles: Wide and smooth here in the beginning. You travel through a basically hardwood forest as the religious complex on the right becomes apparent. They have a farm to tend among their other duties.

0.5 miles: Black River becomes visible on the left.

0.9 miles: Culvert is visible here that allows water to pass through. As of late 1996, it was showing damage to its top surface. Open on the top, it presents a hazard to bike tires, so be careful.

1.1 miles: Diverging path that goes uphill to the right, for an underground AT&T line. A fill then appears.

2.1 miles: Small brook crosses underneath by way of a cast iron culvert about 40 inches in diameter.

2.4 miles: Crossing over a little stream by way of a modern wooden bridge.

3.3 miles: Little bit of a fill with a swamp on the right. Also in this area is Ground Pine (Lycopoduim), which is a protected plant in New Jersey.

3.6 miles: Passing over a timber bridge about 20 feet long with a slow, meandering stream below.

4.0 miles: Coming back into civilization with houses bordering the trail. This is also the end of the line.

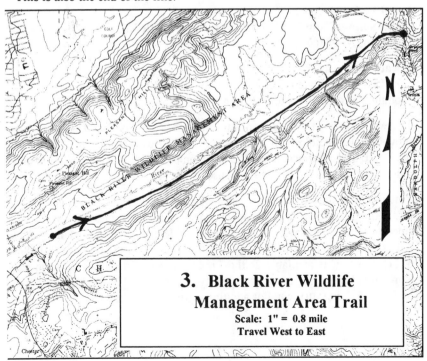

3. Black River Wildlife Management Area Trail
Scale: 1" = 0.8 mile
Travel West to East

4 Capoolong Fish and WMA

Pittstown Branch of the Lehigh Valley Railroad

Endpoints: Quakertown Road in Pittstown to Landsdown Road in
Landsdown
Location: Hunterdon County, Pittstown and Landsdown
Length: 3.7 miles
Surface: Cinder and gravel
Map(s): Pittstown, U.S.G.S. 1:24,000 series
Uses: All non-motorized uses. Horses by permit only.

To get there: Take I-78 to exit 15 (Clinton/Pittstown, 173 East). Take a
left onto Route 513 South at the light at the end of the ramp. Go about 0.4
miles and take left onto Quakertown Road. The trail starts on the left just
after you cross a stream.

Contact:
Division of Fish, Game and Wildlife
P.O. Box 400
Trenton, NJ 08625
609-292-2965

Local Bed & Breakfast:
Seven Springs Farm Bed N Breakfast, 14 Perryville Rd.,
Pittstown, NJ 08867 (908) 735-7675

Local resources for bike repair:
Bike Line, 2002 State Route 31, Clinton, NJ 08809 (908) 638-4488
Mountain Sports, 107 Sidney Rd., Annandale NJ 08801 (908) 735-6244

The was formerly the Pittstown Railroad, a branch from the Lehigh Valley
(now Conrail) mainline, from Lansdown to Pittstown. Today, it is owned by
the DEPE and administered by the Division of Fish, Game and Wildlife as a
wildlife management area and is in use as a trail.

This is a pleasant, flat trail that parallels the Capoolong Creek. It is suitable
for hiking, horses, and off-road bicycles. It is not improved, but has a
smooth, hard cinder base. As in all of New Jersey's Wildlife Management
Areas, horses require an annual permit (Contact Fish & Game at (609) 984-
6211). Parking is available at the Pittstown Post Office, across from the
Hoff Mills Inn which serves good hearty meals, or at The Tack Room, both
on Route 513 in Pittstown. For additional parking, see below.

0.0 miles: Southern terminus at MCI Electric Company.

0.1 miles: Abandoned railroad station (limited parking) behind Towne Upholstery, off 513 south.

0.8 miles: Cross Whitebridge Road, which also has parking. Walk along the road for 0.1 miles and the trail will resume.

1.3 miles: Iron bridge is here with the bridge ties still in place.

1.7 miles: Cross Lower Kingstown Road. Parking available. Walk or ride along road for 0.2 miles past the Superfund Site (former DDT insecticide plant), and pick up the trail on the right before the bridge.

1.9 miles: Trail resumes.

2.3 miles: Small tie bridge across drainage gully. Horses can take the small path to the right up the hill and follow it across the washed out area, back to the trail.

2.7 miles: Cross Kingstown-Sydney Road, and continue past gate.

3.7 miles: Northern terminus at active railroad tracks.

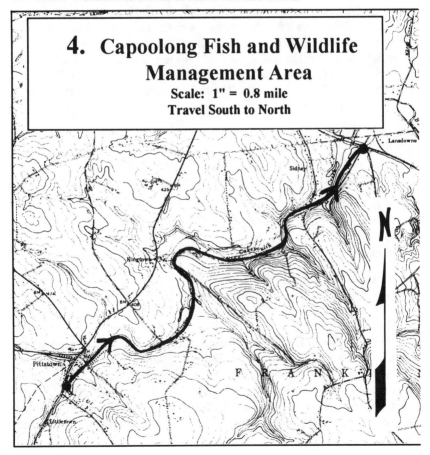

4. Capoolong Fish and Wildlife Management Area

Scale: 1" = 0.8 mile
Travel South to North

5 Columbia Trail

High Bridge Branch of the Central Railroad of New Jersey (CNJ)

Endpoints: Bartley Road in Flanders to Main Street in High Bridge
Location: Morris County and Hunterdon County, townships of Flanders,
Long Valley, Califon, and High Bridge
Length: 16.2 miles
Surface: Dirt, gravel and cinder
Map(s): Chester, Hackettstown, Califon and Highbridge in the U.S.G.S.
1:24,000 series or Newark in the 1:100,000 series.
Uses: All non-motorized uses.

To get there: Take I-80 to exit 27 and then follow Route 206 South to
Flanders. Turn right onto County Route 641, Bartley-Flanders Road. After
about 0.7 miles, take a left. After about 0.4 miles, the road will bend right
and the Morristown & Erie Railroad track will be on the left for about 1.5
miles until you reach the end of the track. A long brick and vinyl-sided
commercial building is on the right and the parking lot is on the left where
there are spaces for about 15 cars. The trail starts in a direct line from the
end of the existing rail.

Contact:
Morris County Park Commission
P.O. Box 1295, Morristown, NJ 07962-1295   973-326-7600
Hunterdon County Parks and Recreation Department   908-782-1158

Local Bed & Breakfast:
The Neighbour House, 143 W. Mill Rd, Long Valley, NJ 07853
908-876-3519
The Publick House, 111 W. Main St., Chester, NJ 07930   908-879-6878

Local resources for bike repair:
Iron Pony Bicycles, 293 Route 206, Flanders, NJ 07836
973-584-2518

The Jersey Central's High Bridge Branch was laid out as 33 miles of single
track and built in the 1860s to connect the mainline at High Bridge with a
series of small branches that led to a number of iron mines. As the years
went by, more than half of the iron ore production of the state of New Jersey
went over the High Bridge Branch. The high point of this traffic was
reached in May, 1882, when 118 cars of ore were shipped over the branch
in one day.

The ore trains were always run as *extras,* one of the train classifications which were usually organized as follows: 1st class were passenger trains, 2nd class were milk trains, 3rd class were general merchandise trains, and all others were considered extras. The rankings were important in order to know which train had priority at a *meet,* which took place at a passing siding where two trains passed each other. The lower class train usually went into a siding and waited for the higher class train to pass. In the early years of the 20th century, there was so much traffic that a great number of passing sidings were built to allow for two-way traffic in several places. The majority of the meets involved a milk train stopping at all the small way stations along the line (this is the origin of the term *milk-run.*)

There was one major customer on line that was a steady source of revenue for the CNJ. The United States Government arsenal at nearby Lake Junction helped keep the branch in the black until nearly the end of operations in the early 1970s.

One of the other major industries on this line was the transportation of ice from Lake Hopatcong to the cities. The railroad had customers in the ice storage business and the railroad itself owned a series of ice-houses that provided a cushion to the private ice-houses as well as a substantial source of revenue for the railroad. Packing the ice into the triple-walled ice-houses and insulating the ice-cakes with straw and hay were important, full-time jobs for many folks in the days before mechanical refrigeration.

But as the traffic on the branch inevitably declined, the CNJ was faced with the hard choices that all the other railroads in the east were facing: How to stop the hemorrhaging caused by unprofitable branch-lines. Larry Lowenthal explained the situation in *The Iron Mine Railroads of New Jersey.*

"In March 1971, as part of its "Blueprint for Survival," the collapsing CNJ decided to eliminate most of its remaining branches in order to preserve a fragment of the system. Under this philosophy of trying to survive as a multiple amputee, the CNJ petitioned the ICC on May 27, 1971, to abandon the High Bridge Branch, Dove & Rockaway RR, and the Mount Hope Mineral RR -- all its remaining Morris County trackage. By then there were reports that Sears, Roebuck & Company was planning a huge warehouse in Mount Olive Township that would generate a good many car-loadings. As a result, the CNJ withdrew the section of its application that concerned the High Bridge and Dove & Rockaway before the remainder of the case was decided on May 26, 1972."

In 1980, the line was severed at Bartley which was just past the Sears warehouse (now Toys R Us), and the portion all the way south to High Bridge was abandoned. The line north from Bartley is now operated by the Morristown & Erie Railroad and caters to the big distribution facility with daily service as needed.

In 1985, an underground natural gas pipeline was installed by the Columbia Gas Company which has been in negotiations with Morris County to turn the trail over to the Park Commissioners. This would then create another gem in the portfolio of trails which Morris County oversees. The section in Hunterdon County is already in operation, though they have some bridges left to bring up to trail standards. Hunterdon expects to begin the final dress-up of the trail and bridge decking in May of 1998.

This trail is also a perfect example of how a community resource such as the local Boy Scouts can become involved in a trail project. Here the High Bridge Council of Scouts regularly has trail maintenance outings from Vernoy to High Bridge. Additionally, every year there is a major Scout Camporee that has a trail and railroad history tie-in.

0.0 miles: Crossing the road at the trail-head and heading south, you'll see the inviting corridor just ahead. It is both interesting and cautionary to note that, until 1970 when the railroad installed warning lights and bells, they used to have many problems with cars hitting the middle of trains at night. Here Bartley Road is in the middle of an S-curve with limited sight distances, so cars came upon the grade crossing very quickly. At night, with no warning lights or bells, many a car came around the bend and hit the train broadside. Use this historical footnote to make your crossing safe.
0.1 miles: Water is on either side, with the stream on the right being the South Branch of the Raritan River. This stream will parallel your ride all the way to High Bridge. A set of railcar wheels known as a "truck" is seen here. Left over from the clean-up of some long-ago derailment, it serves today to graphically prove the trail's railroad origins.
0.2 miles: Agricultural grade crossing.
0.5 miles: A modern 30-foot bridge over Drake's Brook, a tributary of the Raritan River. This structure has old railroad abutments and a modern superstructure consisting of a solid decking of sturdy 3 X 10 planks and steel side rails that are friendly to equestrians. The concrete edging makes for an easy approach.
0.7 miles: Grade crossing of North Four Bridges Road where you'll see an unusual gate which is fairly difficult to cross. Just beyond the road are some old ties, and in a short distance you'll see a battery box that provided the current to activate the warning lights and bells at the grade crossing.

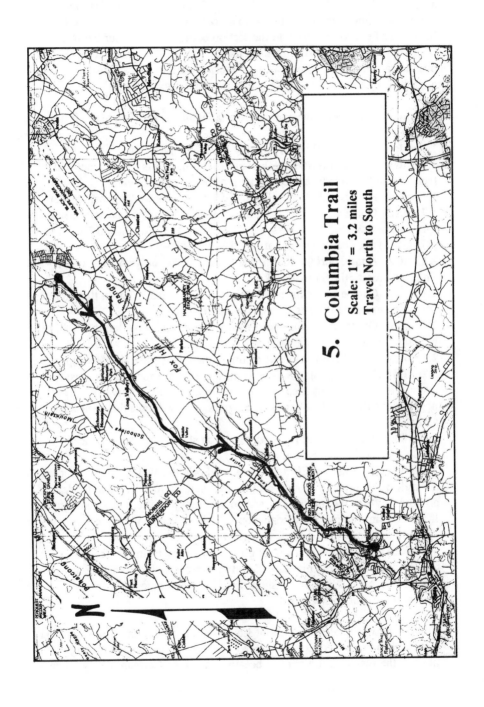

5. Columbia Trail

Scale: 1" = 3.2 miles
Travel North to South

The next mile is the location where a local legend is based. This legend is about the "Hooker Man," a railroad worker from long ago who lost his hand in a train accident and was fitted with a hook. It is said that for the rest of his life, he kept coming back to the section between North Four Bridges Road and Naughright Road, looking for the hand lost in the accident. He usually came at night, armed with a lantern. It is said that a ghostly apparition of a man carrying a lantern can still be seen here.

1.0 miles: Another bridge over the Raritan which is the twin of the last one seen at milepoint 0.5.

1.1 miles: Agricultural grade crossing to a field and a house.

1.2 miles: Here you'll find another similar bridge. This one is about 100 feet long and used to be a deck-girder type in the railroad era.

1.4 miles: Here is a slight cut that doesn't drain very well and can be wet.

1.7 miles: Grade crossing of Naughright Road which is a busy street, so be careful crossing here. Two horse farms are here, the Petit Chaval Farm (876-5518) and the Reiterhof Farm and Stable (876-9063).

2.1 miles: Another bridge which is similar to what you've seen already. This one crosses the Stony Brook.

2.2 miles: Can be wet at times, especially after a steady rain. In this area you'll see some old RR ties stacked up on the right.

2.4 miles: Grade crossing of a dirt road which leads on the left to a fishing hole that the locals say is great.

2.7 miles: River becomes visible again on the left as the trail opens up.

3.2miles: On the right is a 90-degree turn onto a dirt road which must be taken. The trail straight ahead is not open to the public as there are negotiations for a trail easement in progress. You will take this road west and uphill.

3.3 miles: Fairview Road is found here. You should turn left and head south, past the Frazier Steel Company.

3.6 miles: Passing over Electric Brook, and past the Welch Farms complex.

3.8 miles: Going over another bridge, and then the road bends to the left and the RoW for the trail is accessed on the right just after the green house. If you continue on Fairview Road, you will shortly come upon the Washington Township Historical Museum.

3.9 miles: The old two-track deck girder bridge is a primitive crossing with only bridge ties and old planks laid on top. Next is a grade crossing of Fairview Avenue. It is worth a short detour to view some of the lovely period homes and businesses.

You are now in the community of Long Valley, which dates back to 1731 and used to be named Dutch Valley in honor of the country of origin for most of the residents. Later on it became known as German Valley when a group of emigrants left the German state of Saxony to escape religious persecution, heading for the Dutch colony in New Amsterdam (now known as Manhattan, New York). The ship carrying the Germans ran into unfavorable winds and was diverted to Philadelphia. Undaunted, they set out to go overland to New Amsterdam. When they came upon the beautiful vista in this area, they decided to stay here and since they outnumbered the original residents, they of course renamed it as German Valley. During World War I, when any reference to Germany was unpopular, the town was finally renamed Long Valley. Thus it is that this small community has the unique distinction as having three names in only 200 years.

The community became a key railroad town when the Chester Branch was constructed and the ore trains came rumbling through. The junction with the Chester Branch was here, as well as extensive engine servicing facilities, including a turntable. At the turn of the century, when the iron mines in Chester started to reduce production, German Valley reflected the changes with scaled-back facilities. The community was also famous for Schooley's Mountain, one of those special grand resort destinations so common at the turn of the century.

4.0 miles: Triple-track crossing of a small stream. This bridge is a deck girder type and this one also has only bridge ties for decking. The third track led to a coal tipple once part of the Ballantine Building Materials Company. Look for the lumber shed's sliding doors that faced the rail-siding. Closing a few years ago as a result of competition by Home Depot, it is now an antique store. On the right you'll see an abandoned bank that has been converted to the Town Tax office with a drive up window. This was the site of the original Long Valley passenger station. One business from the railroad days is still operational in this neighborhood, Stefan's Dairy Supply, which is still a major supplier to the region's farmers.
4.1 miles: A skating pond is seen on the left. An inclined ramp to a trail neighbor is seen on the right.
4.2 miles: More ties are seen rotting in the woods on the left.
4.8 miles: Grade crossing of a private driveway.
5.0 miles: Another private grade crossing
5.2 miles: Culvert made of two upright stones capped by a cross-piece. Then you come upon a gentle 6-foot cut.
5.6 miles: Now you are on a fill about ten feet tall.
5.7 miles: On another of the ubiquitous bridges as you cross the river once again. This one is a little different in that the abutments are newly pointed with modern cement.
6.1 miles: Blue Crest Farm is on the left.

7.0 miles: Grade crossing of Middle Valley Road. If there has been any rain lately, this area will be muddy. Across the street, you'll find the Burd Used Car Company where Mr. Burd sells mostly old Fords from the 50s, 60s, and 70s. At one time, this village was home to a few creameries and was an important dairy shipping center. The Middle Valley passenger depot was near here, as was the usual freight station, but both were torn down shortly after World War II.

7.2 miles: Another bridge of the same construction you've seen already, but this one is much longer (200 feet), as the trail crosses over the river once again. There is another bridge just ahead that used to span Mallard Cove Road. This was a very unusual bridge that had a concrete center pier in the middle of the road. Unfortunately, the bridge itself used to be only 7 feet high above the road, permitting access only to cars as no trucks of any kind could clear under the peculiar span. It was dismantled in 1975 when the line was shut down. In fact, this was one of the first road improvements after the railroad left. The piers are all that remain.

7.9 miles: Grade crossing of County Route 513, West Mill Road. Across the street, you'll see a commercial wholesale nursery known as Schubert Farm. In railroad circles this area was also known as Crestmoor where a flag-stop station stood, which measured only 6 by 12 feet, the smallest on the line. (A *flag-stop station* was one that literally had a flag for passengers to display to the approaching train. Thus alerted, the engineer would stop and take on those passengers. Normally there would not be a stop.) As of the fall of 1997, the trail makes a slight detour here because the farm has expanded onto the corridor all the way to the next river crossing. To make the detour, take a right onto County Route 513. This situation might change by the time this book is published, as Morris County Parks Commission is working with the farm's owners to reestablish the original RoW.

8.1 miles: Going past Echo Hill Farms with their little private bridge over the Raritan. Just ahead, you'll see what is everyone's childhood memory of a haunted house, a large Victorian house in an advanced state of disrepair, complete with crookedly hanging shutters and a foreboding stance.

8.3 miles: Highway 513 now crosses over the Raritan and then into Hunterdon County. The next left is called Vernoy Road and it is where you'll turn left.

8.7 miles: As you go down the hill on Vernoy, you'll see a lime kiln on the right. Ancient stonework cut into the hill fronting a house with four openings that are similar to four fireplaces. The headers on the openings are old 60-pound rail. Since this area was a big producer of iron ore; it was logical to have some small businesses set up to help supply needed material for processing the ore. Fired lime was used to help purify the ore in the process of making iron.

8.9 miles: Pass over a small automobile bridge which crosses the Raritan. Adjacent to this is a lovely blue house that sits in a perfect setting near the burbling river. The trail will rejoin the road just ahead to the right.

9.0 miles: Here is the start of the Hunterdon County section of the trail and this is the site of the former Vernoy flag-stop station. Hunterdon County will have some signs you'll be seeing along the way. The first one is a large kiosk type that tells you are in the South Branch Reservation, Hunterdon County Park System, Columbia Trail, Tewksbury Township. At the start is a 4 X 4 post about five feet tall which has a 0 on one-side and an 8 on the other side, one of the more visible signposts on the Hunterdon County component, placed every ¼ mile from Vernoy to High Bridge.

9.1 miles: You might find it a little muddy here as you enter a small cut about five feet deep.

9.3 miles: Pass over a culvert that is built of the old-style construction with two stones for sides and one as a cap. More old ties are still visible here as you get into a residential neighborhood. Vernoy Road is next to you, with trail-head parking available.

9.6 miles: Vernoy Street remains a companion on the right. It drifts slowly away to the right and becomes known as Bank Street.

9.8 miles: An interesting old stone and stucco house on the left, then a grade crossing that accesses the houses.

9.9 miles: Hunterdon County mile-marker which says 1 mile on it.

10.6 miles: Here is an old rail-served lumber yard known as Califon Lumber. The gate for the train crew to access the site is still intact.

10.7 miles: You are now entering the small town of Califon. You come upon a 20-foot bridge over a small stream, then the grade crossing of Main Street in Califon.

The restored building on the left, housing the fire department, was the old Waldron's Creamery which was a rail-served customer. Milk production on the order of about 15,000 quarts a day was sent out from this shipper. This was the most important traffic to originate from this charming community. The creamery ran from the 1910s until 1967, spanning three generations of Waldrons. The building is listed on the State and National Register of Historic Places. Note the upper-level freight unloading door with its associated jib crane. The Main Street side of the building shows signs of having a truck freight door where the main entrance is today. Back in 1976, Califon was the second place in the entire state to be recognized by the National and State Registries of Historic Places. The group that organized the support for those projects has evolved to become the Califon Historical Society, whose headquarters is in the old passenger station just ahead. The Society has published an informative, free brochure that describes a walking tour of Califon. A copy can be found at the Califon Book Store on Main Street, 908-832-6686.

CNJ train thundering past the Califon station in the winter of 1940 (photo courtesy of Califon Historical Society)

The Califon station today, now the headquarters for the Califon Historical Society

This community looks like a snap shot from the early part of the century. It is a living example of a rapidly disappearing phenomenon, the small New Jersey town. According to the Califon Historical Society brochure, "no one famous ever lived in Califon and nothing of historical importance ever happened here. Yet it is a time capsule of the lives of the hardworking men and women, farmers and trades-people who built it."

10.8 miles: Grade crossing at County Road 512 (also known as Academy Street), with Railroad Street running parallel to the trail. The Califon Station is intact and is the only stone passenger station on the branch. It seems that the residents of Califon were unhappy with the railroad's typical wooden station, so the town made an arrangement to bring cut-stone to the site and the railroad would construct a more fitting station. Built with a hip-roof providing about four feet of overhang, the station has been restored by the Califon Historical Society for their offices, and it contains much in the way of local history. (Open on the 1st and 3rd Sunday of the month in the afternoons from May through December. Call 908-832-0878 for more information.) Just past the station is an old wood-working facility with a cyclone-type dust collector on the roof.

11.3 miles: Grade crossing of an access road which leads to an automobile junk yard.

11.7 miles: County sign notes that you are now in Lebanon Township.

12.0 miles: Grade crossing of a driveway. The county post mile marker here says you've gone three miles from the start of the Hunterdon County.

12. 5 miles: Grade crossing at Hoffman's Crossing Road. There was once a flag-stop station located at this site.

12.7 miles: A large meadow lies above the trail on the left and the ground falls away to the right as you come into the Lockwood Gorge area.

12.9 miles: The river is about sixty feet below you on the right and the hillside to the left gets more remote.

13.0 miles: Pass by the County marker denoting 4 miles.

13.5 miles: You are now at the north end of the high-bridge over the gorge. With deck girder construction with a center span, this bridge doesn't have a good improved deck as of early 1998. Still, with bridge ties and planking, it can be crossed but may not be a fun experience for all. Fully enclosed with chain link fencing, but no improved treadway, the bridge is about 260 feet long. It should be improved by late 1998. A sign nearby notes that the most spectacular wreck in the annals of the High Bridge Branch took place on this gorge bridge between Califon and High Bridge on April 18, 1885. Engine # 112 was pulling 45 cars and a caboose when it crashed through the bridge, depositing the accumulated mineral wealth of upper Morris County at the bottom of the South Branch of the Raritan River.

13.55 miles: Site of a former hobo camp on the left is still in-use as evidenced by cooking utensils hanging from the tree branches.

13.6 miles: Now on the other side of the river, the RoW curves around to the right as you pass through a fairly substantial cut.

13.7 miles: Steep embankment down to the river which is now 80+ feet below. You are on a shelf with the mountain rising above on the right.

13.8 miles: Look for the interesting stand of trees on the right growing through some crevices in the rock slide.

14.2 miles: A pleasant waterfall on the right is worth a stop to pause, listen and relax. It cascades through the rocks for 400 feet. You're still on the shelf, but now are over 100 feet above the river.

14.7 miles: Crossing under some power lines where it might be a little muddy. This is where the pipeline leaves the RoW and heads up the hill to the right. You'll notice the surface changing ahead as the cinder installed by the railroad many years ago is intact and undisturbed.

14.9 miles: Steep fill as you approach a bridge over Cokesbury Road. This is another bridge with a less than desirable treadway. It is constructed with original bridge-ties and is a deck girder type of bridge about 30 feet long.

15.0 miles: The trail overlooks one of the oldest Boy Scout Camps in the country, Camp Dill.

15.1 miles: Now you're going through a cut and then quickly you'll be looking out to the left at Lake Solitude, a component of the Raritan River. If you are coming through here in the spring, you might be wondering where all the daffodils came from. The local Boy Scouts from High Bridge's own Troop 149 plant 1,000 bulbs each October, and they've been at it for six years now. If you are traveling through any other time of year, you will wish you came through in the spring.

15.6 miles: On a fill over 70 feet tall with a culvert at the base which allows a stream to get to the Raritan.

15.9 miles: Into a cut and then a neighborhood is seen on each side above as you have entered the community of High Bridge. Thomas Street is the road above. Up until the 1950s, a boxed pony-truss bridge was located here. The boxed pony-truss was a cousin of the more conventional covered bridge in that all the supporting trusses were encased in wood for weather.

16.1 miles: Grade crossing of Mill Street where the neighbors have made the RoW a sort of unofficial street.

16.2 miles: The official end of the trail is located at the grade crossing for Main Street. A dedication sign is posted at the trail-head. Across the street is public parking for trail-head users. This was the site of the old High Bridge rail yard and was upgraded with a crushed stone surface and landscaping in May of 1998. On the left side of the parking lot you will see a track curving away to the left. This eventually leads to the New Jersey Transit mainline and station at High Bridge where the commuter line heads east towards New York City.

6 Delaware & Raritan Canal State Park

Bel-Del Division of the Pennsylvania Railroad

Endpoints: Bridge Street in Frenchtown to Parkside Avenue in Trenton
Location: Hunterdon and Mercer Counties, towns of Frenchtown,
Stockton, Lambertville, Titusville, West Trenton, and Trenton
Length: 29.3 miles
Surface: Cinder and Asphalt
Map(s): Frenchtown, Lumberville, Stockton, Lambertville, Pennington,
and Trenton West in the U.S.G.S. 1:24,000 series.
Uses: Non-motorized uses except horses.

To get there: This trail starts at Frenchtown, which is about 10 miles west
of Flemington, on the shore of the Delaware River on Route 12. Parking is
at the corner of River Road and Bridge Street, just south of the bridge that
goes over the Delaware River to Ulherstown, Pennsylvania.

Contact:
Superintendent, D & R Canal State Park
625 Canal Road, Somerset, NJ 08873-7309   732-873-3050

Local Bed & Breakfast:
Inn of the Hawke, 74 S Union St., Lambertville, NJ 08530   609 397-9555
Hunterdon House, 12 Bridge St., Frenchtown, NJ 08825   908-996-3632
York Street House B&B, 42 York St., Lambertville, NJ 08530
609-397-3007

Local resources for bike repair/rentals:
Economy Bicycle Shop, 31 George Dye Rd., Trenton, NJ 08690.
609-586-0150
Freeman's Bicycle Shop, 52 Bridge Street, Frenchtown, NJ 08825.
908-996-7712
Wheel Fine, 639 Brunswick Pike, Lambertville, NJ 08530   609-397-3403

There are many kiosks along the current trail which describe the local
history. The 66-mile-long Delaware & Raritan Canal was planned to be 75
feet wide and 8 feet deep, and was hand-dug by Irish immigrants in 1834.
There was a great labor shortage in the early 1800s, so contractors brought
in many thousand laborers from Ireland. The rate of $1-a-day was a large
sum of money for men who had nothing in their homeland.

Tranquil view of the D & R Canal Trail

With 14 locks, the canal was operated as an inland water-way between the Delaware and Raritan Rivers. Its primary traffic was coal barges pulled by mules along a tow-path to the New York City market. In March, 1836, the Belvidere Delaware Railroad Company was incorporated as one of the earliest railroads in the country and one of a small handful that shared the RoW with a canal. Plagued by financial uncertainty in the markets, the Bel-Del, as it was known to the locals, did not reach north to Phillipsburg until 1854. It was engineered and built by Ashbel Welsh, a prominent citizen of Lambertville. Because Welsh was a very religious man, the railroad's first employee timetable stipulated that liquor was expressly prohibited and that the Sabbath was to be observed.

By 1857, the line reached Mauch Chunk (now called Jim Thorpe) in Pennsylvania, and at the same time, a 12-mile branch to Ringoes (today's Black River & Western Railroad), became operational. In addition to coal, the Bel-Del became a carrier of iron ore from mines in northwest New Jersey to the Hewitt & Cooper Iron Mill in Trenton. With Welsh's natural affinity to Lambertville, this community was chosen over Trenton to be the site of the extensive engine and yard facilities.

For decades, the Bel-Del hosted many exclusive name trains, along with their Pullman diner cars. Here the patrons were treated to a spectacular vista of scenery unparalleled in the mid-Atlantic region. After 1932, the canal was abandoned by its parent company, the Pennsylvania Railroad. In 1933, the Trenton area of the canal was partially filled-in as part of a WPA Project. The end of passenger service came in 1960 when the Pennsy, who had operated the Bel-Del as one of their divisions since 1878, determined the service to be a loss.

Today the water itself is the resource for many of the communities along the way. It is still part of the state's water supply system, with some being sold to farmers for irrigation and some sold to municipalities for drinking water. One million people in New Jersey use D & R Canal water for their daily supply. The Delaware & Raritan (D&R) Canal is one of the country's oldest yet best preserved canals.

This corridor became a state park in 1974. Today, the Delaware & Raritan Canal State Park is one of the most heavily used state parks in New Jersey. It is open for hikers, joggers, and bicyclists from Lawrence Township to New Brunswick, and from Trenton to Raven Rock on the abandoned Bel-Del Railroad RoW. The canal is stocked with fish every spring and camping is allowed on Bull's Island. The trail starts in downtown Frenchtown, which is a lively small town with some gourmet restaurants and equally impressive B&Bs. You might want to check out the American Loafers Bistro and the Bridge Cafe.

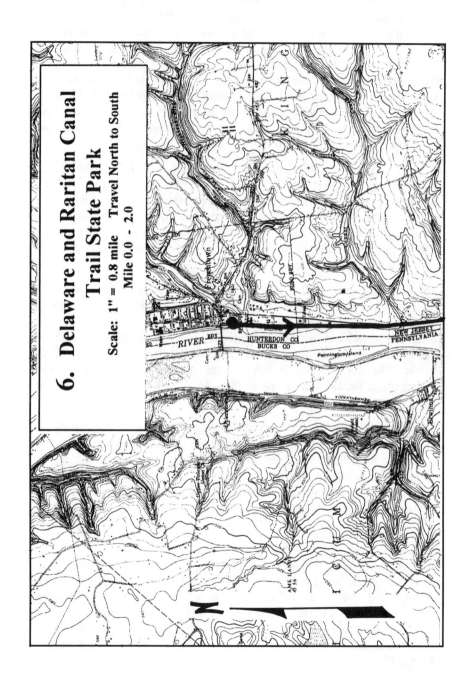

6. Delaware and Raritan Canal Trail State Park

Scale: 1" = 0.8 mile   Travel North to South
Mile 0.0 - 2.0

0.0 miles: The old Frenchtown passenger station on the left has been converted to a residence and painted white. You will be going across an unusual pair of fully landscaped small bridges about 25 feet long which pass over a pair of small streams, the Neshisakawick and Little Neshisakawick.
0.3 miles: Passing through a smattering of houses. The neighbors apparently cut the grass that grows along the trail. Bravo!
0.5 miles: Grade crossing of Washington Street which leads to Old River Road. Look for the railroad ties stacked off to the side just before the grade crossing. Note the house on stilts. The owner must be familiar with the flood cycle of the Delaware.
0.7 miles: Here is something unique. Signage here indicates that the area adjacent to the trail is a hazardous site and you must stay on the trail. It seems that the areas beyond the normal treadway for the trail were contaminated by industrial activity in the days before environmental concerns. Concrete mile marker here denotes 37 miles, and the ubiquitous Purple Loosestrife grows abundantly here.
0.8 miles: Entering a dense forest which blocks the view of the river.
0.9 miles: A small chemical factory here was rail-served at one time.
1.0 miles: Kingwood Fishing Access site is here. This is considered to be a good entry point for the trail with easy access to the parallel Route 29. This site is managed by the New Jersey Department of Environmental Protection, Division of Fish Game and Wildlife. Good parking area.
1.4 miles: Here is a small, concrete octagon passenger waiting station or railroad worker's structure. It certainly has seen better days.

This octagon concrete structure on the D & R Canal Trail originally served waiting passengers or workers who maintained a section of the old Bel-Del Railroad

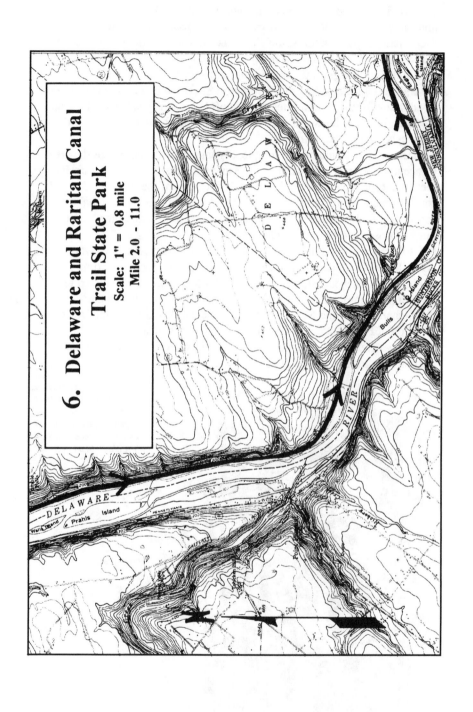

6. Delaware and Raritan Canal Trail State Park

Scale: 1" = 0.8 mile

Mile 2.0 - 11.0

2.7 miles: Picnic table is situated here to take advantage of the beautiful river vistas.

3.5 miles: Outlet to Route 29 and another picnic table. Look for the old rail visible here as well as some ancient ties. This was most likely a double track area to facilitate passing of trains going in different directions.

3.8 miles: Concrete mile-marker here dates to the Pennsylvania Railroad dynasty. It's marked as 28 miles to the south and 40 miles to the north.

4.1 miles: Another access point to Route 29, and the river diverges away from the trail here.

4.5 miles: Route 29 is directly adjacent to you and more ties are visible here. Some cliffs are looming above the road beyond. Look at the trees nearer the river which have sustained damage from some flood of years gone by. It is evident that the flood level was about 25-28 feet above the normal levels.

4.8 miles: The mile-marker here says 27 and 41.

5.1 miles: Going into the first cut here, though not of a significant height or length.

5.5 miles: More old ties are stockpiled here.

5.9 miles: Mile-marker 26 and 42.

6.9 miles: Mile-marker 25 and 43.

7.2 miles: Interesting and unusual stone retaining wall seen here on the left is very intricate, highly detailed, and constructed of large trap-rock.

7.4 miles: Level with the adjacent Route 29, there is a gate to keeps cars out. An old concrete curb on the right is of railroad heritage, perhaps a platform for a passenger station. Other footings of structures are evidence of a water tower and perhaps a freight house. This area was known as Byram on the railroad maps of years ago. You head into the woods again.

7.5 miles: A small residential road with a cluster of houses has appeared between you and the river.

7.9 miles: A grade crossing here allows the road to cross the right-of-way. Note the wood still in the grade crossing, the battery box, and the metal structure which was the base of the grade crossing warning light.

8.1 miles: Interesting series of poles here: 40 inches tall and 4-sided with notches. These served as poles for a barbed wire fence line of years ago. Made of concrete, they were built to last. Look for the home-painted ones further ahead.

8.4 miles: Grade crossing marked as an access point for river rescue crews.

8.6 miles: The canal has appeared between you and the river. This is the official start of the "feeder canal trail." The dam on the Delaware River at Lumberville is just ahead.

8.8 miles: Going over one of the numerous culverts, this one still has a rail in place.

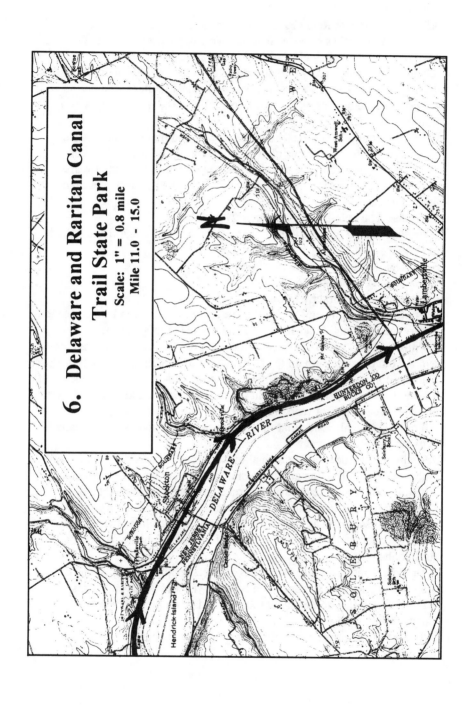

6. Delaware and Raritan Canal Trail State Park

Scale: 1" = 0.8 mile

Mile 11.0 - 15.0

9.0 miles: Concrete platform on the left is all that remains of the Bull Island Passenger Station. Interestingly, a pay telephone is still nearby. A parking area and canoe launch is part of the complex. Take the side tour into the park and check out the bridge over the Delaware.

9.2 miles: On a fill above Route 29 on the left. Farm fields are viewed just beyond the highway.

10.4 miles: Many bulldozed ties lie on the right. Stacked like firewood, they are a constant reminder of the old railroad days.

11.3 miles: Deck girder bridge with nice railings traverses a stream known as Lochatong Creek which feeds the canal. You're likely to come upon some fishermen here.

The Prallsville Mill complex is one of the most photographed scenes in New Jersey.

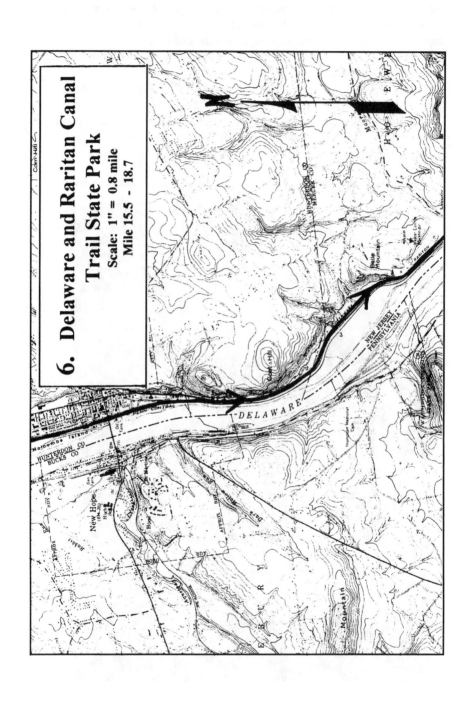

6. Delaware and Raritan Canal Trail State Park

Scale: 1" = 0.8 mile
Mile 15.5 - 18.7

11.8 miles: Here is Prallsville Mill, named after the owner, John Prall, who developed the site in 1794. He enlarged an original lumber operation into a gristmill which milled linseed oil and plaster. The original gristmill burned in 1874 because of a spark provided by a passing Bel-Del locomotive. The complex was rebuilt, enlarged, and operated until 1947. The state acquired the property and the Delaware River Mill Society slowly restored the complex, the only remaining multiple milling operation in the entire state. The feeder canal crosses the main channel here, known as Wickecheoke Creek. Some pressure-treated fencing is here as you cross over the deck-girder bridge which has the deck filled-in with stone.

11.9 miles: Antique cast-iron grade crossing sign is here as well as another one of those small octagon shaped shelters. A kiosk here describes the D&R Canal as the big ditch constructed between the years of 1831-34 at a cost of $3,000,000 and the lives of many of the Irish immigrant laborers.

12.3 miles: Grade crossing of a street. Wooden timbers are still in the road.

12.5 miles: Grade crossing in Stockton at highly urban Ferry Street near Railroad Street, where a passenger station still stands. A sign nearby says the railroad operated through here from 1857 to 1976.

12.6 miles: Back on the trail and out of the station area, the RoW opens up a bit and the neighboring houses are farther back from the trail.

12.8 miles: As you get into a marshy area with fewer houses, you see a signal box and telegraph pole with insulators intact.

13.0 miles: Derelict signal box is on the right, becoming surrounded by the vegetation. A deck-girder bridge over a slow moving stream which is the canal now on the left side of the trail.

13.4 miles: Crossing over an enhanced culvert which is built of concrete and landscaped for 50 feet on each side.

14.2 miles: A railroad siding has appeared on the left. This leads to a quarry on the other side at Mt. Gilboa. The siding is on a fill above the trail and it actually doubles to become two tracks. One of these tracks is a passing siding which allowed for intra-plant switching without fouling the main track. Badly grown in, it has some telegraph poles for company.

14.7 miles: Back to single track siding now, and then under Route 202 which leads across the Delaware River into New Hope, Pennsylvania.

14.9 miles: Grade crossing that is within the complex of a gravel yard/salt storage area. Some old railroad cars are here also: an old Penn-Central (PC) baggage car, a New Jersey Transit E-7 #48, first generation locomotive, a stainless-steel passenger car. Another railroad track has appeared. The switch is in-place, not spiked, and set to the diverging path, which is how the old passenger equipment got here. (*Spiking a switch* means to hammer in large nails or spikes to prevent the switch from being used. This is an effective way to make sure no traffic is allowed to go on the diverging side.)

Lambertville Passenger Station, now a popular restaurant

15.5 miles: Lumber yard is across the canal from the trail. Another railroad electronics cabinet (probably for grade crossing signals) is also found here.

15.6 miles: Parking lot with whistle marker still intact. An octagon waiting station is here in the parking lot of the River Horse Brewery. In addition to housing a micro-brewery, the complex also contains a health club.

16.0 miles: Downtown Lambertville, New Jersey, where a grade crossing is encountered with a wooden bridge over the canal. The Lambertville Passenger Station is here and has been converted to a restaurant. The adjacent street is appropriately called Bridge Street, leading across the river to New Hope, PA. This twin-town area is a great place to stop and check out real downtowns have been preserved and nurtured. Lambertville's attractions include excellent restaurants, book stores, antique shops and historical attractions. Call the Chamber of Commerce at 609-397-0055 for a great brochure. Similar sights exist across the river at New Hope, but here you can find a tourist railroad powered by a steam engine. The New Hope and Ivyland Railroad has a full range of activities at their headquarters in downtown New Hope. Call 215-862-2332 for more info.

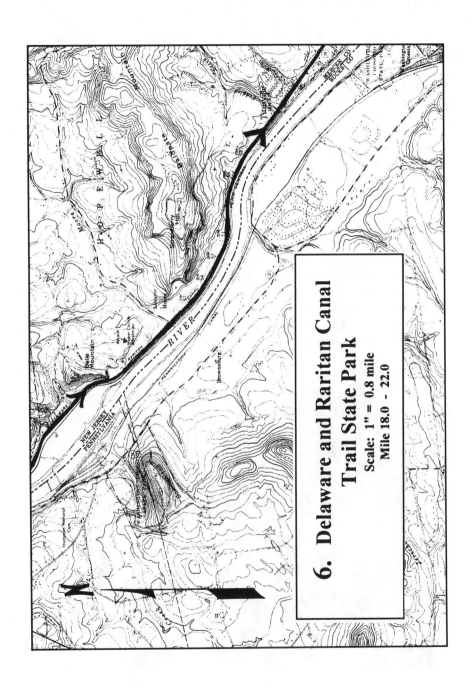

6. Delaware and Raritan Canal Trail State Park

Scale: 1" = 0.8 mile

Mile 18.0 – 22.0

16.1 miles: An outfall for the canal is seen here. This allows excess water to pass out of the canal. Some houses are right on the canal tow-path in this area, while across the canal, is the still active railroad known as the Black River & Western. The BR&W stores some maintenance of way equipment on their line here. *Maintenance of way (MoW) equipment* is usually some old and worn-out rolling-stock that is used to transport personnel, tools and material to job sites. Other types of MoW equipment are specialized track laying or maintaining machinery.

16.9 miles: A dam over the Delaware River is seen here. Not too tall, it nonetheless makes for a memorable sight with fishermen usually in the area. The canal on the left is significantly higher than the river.

17.6 miles: A grade crossing with a kiosk here describes a fire in one of the mills of Lambertville.

18.2 miles: A large meadow off to the right has come between you and the river. Looking to the left, you'll see Belle Mountain and the Mercer County Correction Center.

18.5 miles: An access road for the field crosses the towpath at this point.

19.2 miles: A derelict railroad drawbridge is seen here. With deck girder construction and only one span, it was hinged at the road side and the towpath side would rise and swing away. A bent timber trestle approach is still in place on the canal towpath side. *Bent timber trestle* is a series of Ms built of large timbers and when combined together, make for a strong and relatively cheap bridge.

Rehabilitated old rail-served industry in downtown Lambertville

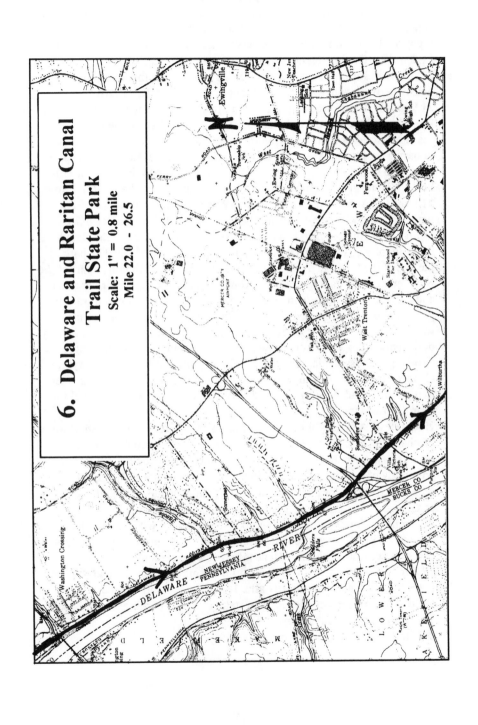

6. Delaware and Raritan Canal Trail State Park

Scale: 1" = 0.8 mile

Mile 22.0 - 26.5

19.5-19.7 miles: Elevated trackage here is part of another bent timber trestle which raises the track to span the canal by another deck girder bridge which stood about 8 feet above the canal. There is a quarry across the highway that the railroad used to serve. The hill itself is Strawberry Hill.

21.2 miles: Grade crossing of an access road to the canal.

21.6 miles: Interesting stone arch bridge which leads to a smattering of houses between you and the river that are accessed by River Drive.

21.9 miles: Grade crossing of Church Street in the village of Titusville. A kiosk here notes that the old Church Street Bridge, like all the others over the canal, used to open, allowing the boat traffic to pass. Each bridge used to have a bridge tender who lived in an adjacent house. Here at Titusville there also used to be a passenger station for the railroad. Evidence is still here in the form of curbing for the platform and a wider than normal RoW.

22.9 miles: You are now passing into Washington Crossing State Park, named of course for being the location where on Christmas Eve, 1776, George Washington led a force of the American Army across the Delaware River in long boats to attack the Hessian garrison at Trenton. The park is the site of the landing. Today this is a large and well maintained part of the New Jersey State Park system, and you will find parking, easy river access and rest room facilities. Some delis are also nearby as well if you want to get a bite to eat and sit under the trees for a while. Note the pedestrian walkway bridge over the adjacent highway which leads to the vast majority of the park's property. Across the river is the community of Washington's Crossing, Pennsylvania, which is accessed by the nearby bridge carrying County Route 546. Also in this area, the Washington Crossing Passenger Station of the old Bel-Del Railroad once stood here, as well as a hotel for railroad travelers.

23.4 miles: A footing for a home signal is seen here. A *Home Signal* was a mechanical device that let the engineer know if the section of track ahead (in this case a passenger station) was occupied. This would alert him of the possibility of meeting another train and which track and speed to use.

23.9 miles: Look for an interesting brown-stone ledge on the left side of the canal.

24.4 miles: You are now coming upon a Par Course with 15 exercise stations. With all the stations here fairly new and in good condition, this course is compact with the distances between the stations around 150 feet.

25.3 miles: Viewable here is a metal mile-marker of the railroad days. It notes 61 miles, and then shortly after is a grade crossing for the access road to the river. This is Scudder Falls, a state park with parking for trail use. The bridge overhead is Interstate 95.

26.2 miles: Grade crossing of Route 634.

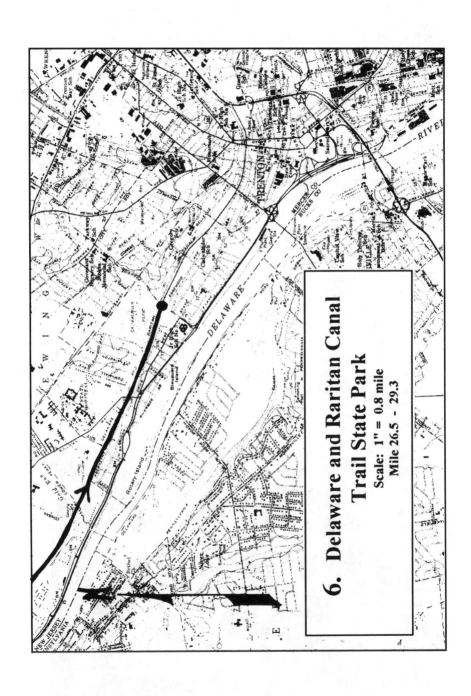

6. Delaware and Raritan Canal Trail State Park

Scale: 1" = 0.8 mile

Mile 26.5 - 29.3

26.6 miles: Entering the village of Greensburgh. Look for the interesting signage on the kiosk located here. There used to be station here as well as an extensive array of track. At the intersection of Wilburtha Road and the D & R Canal, the area was once known as Wilburtha. This unusual name came from the Fisk's, a wealthy family in the mid-1880s who had a son named Wilbur and a daughter named Bertha. Their home today is known as the Villa Victoria Academy and the estate is on the right near Route 634. Near the grade crossing for Wilburtha Road is a battery box for the grade crossing signals. On the right is a railroad siding, still intact for the Trenton Stone Company which is a neighbor to the trail. Many a car of brown-stone left from this site to go to New York and Philadelphia to construct brown-stone apartments. On the left is property of the New Jersey State Hog Farm.

27.3 miles: Another metal mile-marker is seen here. This one says 5 miles on one side (to Trenton station) and the other side says 63 miles. You are crossing under the electrified commuter rail line that used to by owned by the Reading Railroad. Today it is owned by the South East Pennsylvania Transit Authority. This deck girder bridge used to have quadruple tracks, though it is only double-tracked today.

27.5 miles: You are now coming upon a "W" marker. This means whistle. The engineer would blow the whistle for the crossing ahead at Lower Ferry Road. Just ahead is the Trenton Country Club which actually bisects the canal and the trail.

28.5 miles: The canal is carried by an aqueduct over Sullivan Way, a road that passes underneath.

29.3 miles: A pedestrian walk bridge over the canal and another aqueduct over a boulevard below known as Parkside Avenue. This is the effective end of the trail.

One of the few remaining railroad bridges over the D & R Canal

7 Edgar Felix Memorial Trail
Eastern end of Penn Central Railroad's Freehold Secondary

Endpoints: North Main St., Manasquan, to Hospital Road, Wall Township.
Location: Monmouth County, Wall Township
Length: 3.6 miles
Surface: Asphalt
Map(s): Asbury Park, U.S.G.S 1:24,000 series
Uses: Non-motorized uses except horses.

To get there: Take exit 98 off of the Garden State Parkway to Route 34
South. Go approximately 2 miles and then take County Route 524 east (also
known as Atlantic Ave). You will shortly come upon Route 35. Continue
past this about 9 blocks, and then turn right onto North Main Street. After
one block, you will see a gas station on the right and next to this is the trail-
head. Park across the street in the municipal lot.

Contact:
Wall Township Parks & Recreation
2700 Allaire Road, Wall, NJ 07719. 732-449-8444

Local Bed & Breakfast:
Pier House Guests, 27 Ocean Avenue, Point Pleasant Beach, NJ 08742.
732-295-0180
Normandy Inn, 21 Tuttle Avenue, Spring Lake, NJ 07762. 732-449-7172
Sea Crest By the Sea, 19 Tuttle Avenue, Spring Lake, NJ 07762.
732-449-9031
Spring Lake Inn, 104 Salem Avenue, Spring Lake, NJ 07762.
732-449-2010

Local resources for bike repair:
Manasquan Bicycle Service Center, 128 Main St., Manasquan, NJ 08736.
732-223-2444

This trail is part of what originated as the Freehold and Jamesburg
Agricultural Railroad in the 1800s. When fully built, it ran from Monmouth
Junction (west of Jamesburg), right through the Jamesburg business district,
then through Freehold, Farmingdale, Allenwood, Manasquan, and finally
terminated at the New York and Long Branch (now the New Jersey Coast
Line). The road eventually became part of the Penn-Central (PC) System.

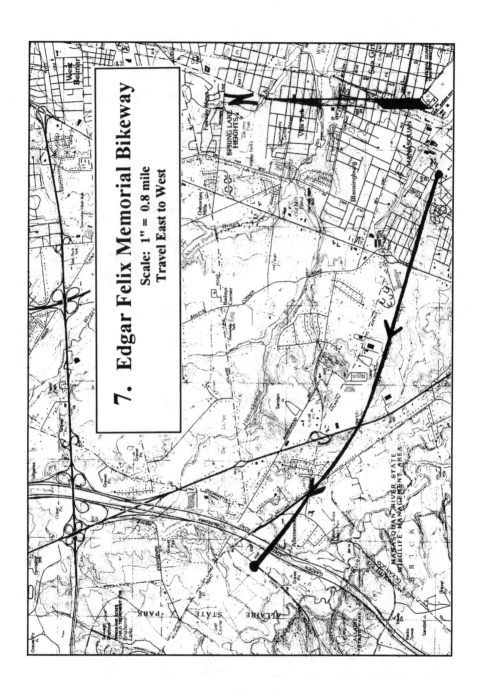

7. Edgar Felix Memorial Bikeway

Scale: 1" = 0.8 mile
Travel East to West

Most of this road, from Monmouth Junction to Farmingdale, is still active as Conrail's Freehold Secondary and might see future commuter service. The portion east of Farmingdale was abandoned by the PC and sold to Jersey Central Power and Light, which sold it to Wall Township. The Felix Bike Path was developed on the section from Hospital Road to Main Street in Manasquan in 1971 and 1972. The remainder towards Farmingdale is mostly within the boundaries of Allaire State Park and is open to public use. It is described in Ride # 8.

The Felix Bike Path is maintained by the Wall Township Public Works Department which makes periodic patching and cleaning runs, and has resurfaced portions. The trail is in very good condition; it has only three grade crossings and none are major. Starting at the Manasquam end is recommended because of the abundant services available. ATM machines, restaurants, and stores are on Main Street. A cautionary note: This trail is somewhat unique compared to other paved trails in that it does not have ballards that prevent unwanted vehicles from entering the trail, only signs that warn of NO MOTOR BIKES.

0.0 miles: A canopy of hardwood trees provides some shade as you start this pleasant urban/suburban trail. The little stream meandering through the area is Judas Creek. You will notice a grade uphill, heading away from the ocean.

0.4 miles: Bordering the trail on the left is Orchard Park, with its tennis courts. An access point to the right leads to a farm.

0.7 miles: Passing under Route 35. This bridge dates from the days of the railroad.

0.8 miles: The surroundings have opened up now and you are passing through what used to be an apple orchard, though it is now overgrown.

1.0 miles: On a fill about 15-18 feet tall and passing a condo development, then back into the woods.

1.6 miles: Passing by a well-maintained mobile home park. Gas and electric utilities are sharing the right of way here also.

1.7 miles: Out of the hardwood forest and into a scrub pine area. There is a small cut about 10 feet deep.

1.9 miles: Going past a few modern commercial establishments that include a Budweiser distributorship and an Airborne Express terminal.

2.1 miles: The grade has flattened out just as you pass under Route 34. Its bridge dates from the rail era.

2.2 miles: The area becomes more wooded again.

2.5 miles: Another residential neighborhood on the right.

2.6 miles: A small side street on the right has an access point to the trail.

2.7 miles: Grade crossing of Ramshorn Drive, which makes an oblique angle, so be careful. This trail is somewhat unique compared to other paved trails in that it does not have ballards that prevent unwanted vehicles from entering the trail, only signs that warn of NO MOTOR BIKES. A small park is here for your resting pleasure. Across the street is the Allenwood General Store which sells food as well as an eclectic mix of antiques. A plywood sign is here that shows the layout of the trail. Majestic Aerotech, a modern machine shop across the trail, shows signs of having been a rail-served industry in its past life.

3.2 miles: This area also gives hints that it may have been the site of a small rail yard.

3.3 miles: A small pond on the right is visible before you cross over the Garden State Parkway. A bike bridge has been built to take you across. With its nicely arched spans, it makes for an interesting way to cross the busy interstate.

3.6 miles: Small parking lot is here to serve trail users. The New Jersey Water Treatment Authority Manasquan Water Supply System building is ahead across the street which is known as Hospital Road. Just beyond the Water Treatment facility, the trail gets a soft surface and the birds become plentiful. Look for the occasional tie still found in the area. The Edgar Felix trail will end at the Golf Course, and the Freehold and Jamesburg Trail starts in that area. (See Ride # 8)

The start of the Edgar Felix Bicycle Path

8 Freehold and Jamesburg Trail
Penn-Central's Freehold Secondary

Endpoints: Hospital Road, Allenwood, to Route 547, Farmingdale
Location: Southeast Monmouth County, Wall Township, and Farmingdale.
Length: 4.5 miles
Surface: Gravel and dirt
Maps: Asbury Park and Farmingdale in the U.S.G.S.1:24,000 series, or Trenton in the 1:100,000 series.
Uses: All non-motorized uses.

To get there: Take the Garden State Parkway to Exit 98, to Route 34 South. Take a right at the first light onto Allenwood Road, and then follow signs to Allaire State Park. In 0.7 miles, at the T intersection turn right onto Atlantic Avenue. In 0.3 miles, turn left onto Hospital Road. The trail will be on your right in 0.2 miles, with parking space for four cars on the left. This start point is actually the end point of the Edgar Felix Trail (see Ride # 7). The nearby Allaire State Park contains a nineteenth century iron plantation. They also host the Pine Creek Railroad (732- 938-5524), which runs short steam train excursions.

Contact:
Allaire State Park
P.O. Box 220, Farmingdale, NJ 07727.
732-938-2371

Local Bed & Breakfast:
Pier House Guests, 27 Ocean Avenue, Point Pleasant Beach, NJ 08208.
732-295-0180
Normandy Inn, 21 Tuttle Ave., Spring Lake NJ. 07762. 732-449-7172
Sea Crest by the Sea, 19 Tuttle Ave., Spring Lake, NJ 07762.
732-449-9031
Spring Lake Inn, 104 Salem Ave., Spring Lake NJ 07762. 732-449-2010

Local resources for bike repair/rentals:
Brielle Cyclery, 205 Union Avenue, Route 71, Brielle NJ 08730.
732-528-9121

The following information is from a brochure published by the New Jersey RailTrails, a state-wide non-profit group that works to turn abandoned railroads into multi-use public trails. Information about joining is available by writing to P.O. Box 23, Pluckemin, NJ, 07978, 215-340-9974.

This trail is part of what originated as the Freehold and Jamesburg Agricultural Railroad in the 1800s. When fully built, it ran from Monmouth Junction (west of Jamesburg), went right through the Jamesburg business district, then through Freehold, Farmingdale, Allenwood, Manasquan, and terminated at the New York and Long Branch (now the North Jersey Coast Line.) The road eventually became part of the Penn Central System. Most of this, from Monmouth Junction to Farmingdale, is still active as Conrail's Freehold Secondary, and might see future commuter service. The portion east of Farmingdale was abandoned by the Penn Central and sold to Jersey Central Power and Light, which sold it to Wall Township. Part of this latter piece, from Hospital Road to Main Street in Manasquam, has been developed as the Edgar Felix Memorial Trail. This trail (the F&J) is the remainder in the middle, which is now inside Allaire State Park.

This trail has some interruptions and is not marked as a completely independent trail. However, it still can be easily followed and it provides a very scenic route. Two detours (described later) are necessary, around the golf course and another around I-195, both of which cut the corridor. Please note that bicycles are not permitted in Allaire Village or on the immediate adjacent trails. To visit the village area by bicycle, enter on the access road and check with the ranger.

0.0 miles: Starting at the Hospital Road end and heading west towards Farmingdale. The Edgar Felix Trail (see Ride # 7) heads east from here.
0.4 miles: Skirt just to the right of the golf course green, toward the corner of the trees ahead.
0.5 miles: Turn right at the trees, following the trail along the right edge. Turn left into the woods. From here, follow the Red Trail.
0.7 miles: Cross the entrance to the Spring Meadow Golf Course.
0.8 miles: Enter Allaire Road parking lot. Head to the opposite side, toward your left.
0.9 miles: Leave parking lot between two wood barriers. Follow straight trail.
1.0 miles: Turn right to return to the railroad right-of-way.
1.5 miles: Turn left on Allaire Road. The Pine Creek Railroad is just to your left which is accessed through the park.
1.6 miles: Entrance to Allaire State Park.
2.3 miles: Turn right on Red Trail, soon after passing under I-195.
2.6 miles: Turn right at first 4-way trail crossing.
2.8 miles: Go left to continue down the abandonment.
3.7 miles: Continue straight when a road bears left, and straight again when another road then bears right.
4.1 miles: Cross Hurley Pond Road.

4.3 miles: Continue straight when the trail turns right, under the power lines.

4.5 miles: Trail ends at Route 547. The Farmingdale business district is one mile down Route 547 to the right.

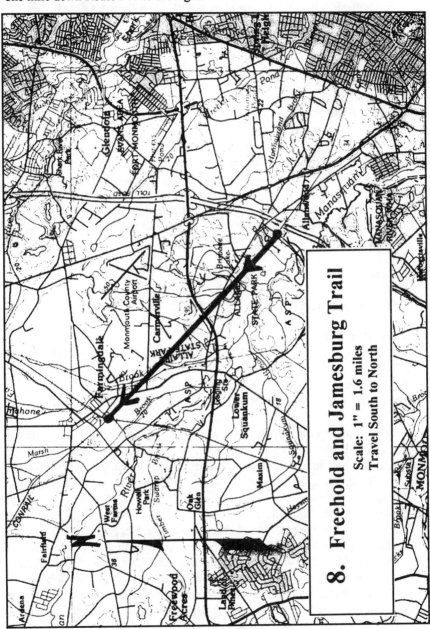

8. Freehold and Jamesburg Trail

Scale: 1" = 1.6 miles
Travel South to North

9 Hamburg Mountain WMA

Hanford Branch of the New York, Susquehanna & Western Railroad

Endpoints: Ogden Way, Ogdensburg, to just west of Beaver Lake Road, Franklin.
Location: Sussex County, townships of Ogdensburg and Franklin.
Length: 2.6 miles
Surface: Cinder
Map(s): Franklin, U.S.G.S. 1:24,000 series
Uses: All non-motorized uses. Horses by permit only

To get there: From State Route 23, proceed to Franklin, and turn at the traffic light onto Sussex County Route 517 south. Proceed 1.5 miles south into Ogdensburg to a small dirt parking area on the left, a few feet north of Ogden Way. This marks the beginning of the trail, which climbs from 700 feet above sea level at the parking area, to 990 feet at its terminus at Beaver Lake Junction, 2.6 miles away.

Contact:
Division of Fish, Game and Wildlife
P.O. Box 400, Trenton, NJ 08625. 973-292-2965

Local Bed & Breakfast:
Sullivan's Gas Light Inn, 382 Rte. 23, Franklin, NJ 07416. 973-209-9723

Local resources for bike repair:
Bike Stop, Route 206, Newton, NJ 07860. 973-579-5434

Franklin and Ogdensburg are known to geologists throughout the world for the unusual minerals which have been mined here for over two hundred years. During the height of mining operations, the Hanford Branch of the New York, Susquehanna & Western Railroad was built through the Hamburg mountains to service the New Jersey Zinc Company mines in Ogdensburg and Franklin, as well as towns north and west of here. Zinc and iron ores were transported from the mines along this branch to the NYS&W's mainline at Beaver Lake Junction, and then onto the smelters which would refine ores into metal. Although the mines are no longer active, the Hanford Branch which served them has gained new life as part of the Hamburg Mountain Wildlife Management Area. Visitors to this site will find a scenic trail with a mild uphill climb which is suitable for hiking, bicycles, and horses (with permits.)

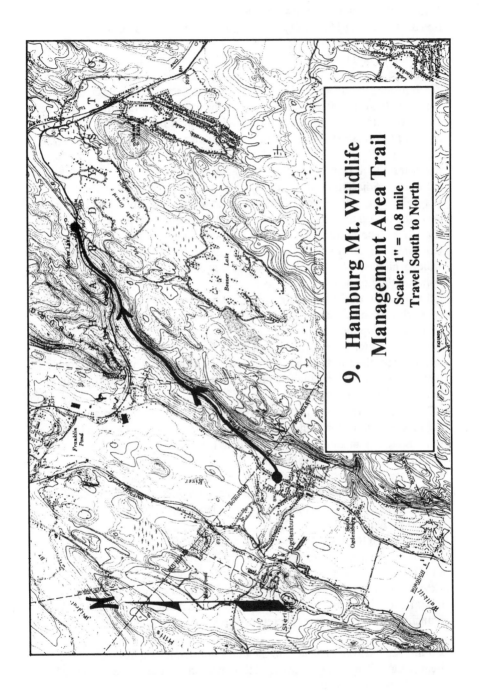

9. Hamburg Mt. Wildlife Management Area Trail

Scale: 1" = 0.8 mile

Travel South to North

Two nearby attractions illustrate the once prosperous mining industry in this area. Sterling Hill in Ogdensburg, once a major producer of zinc ore, conducts tours of the mine at 1 PM and 3 PM daily, with an additional tour of the mine at 11 AM on weekends. The mine is closed on weekdays in December and March, and completely closed during January and February. For information call (973) 209-7212. Those interested in geology can visit the Franklin Mineral Museum in Franklin and view Franklinite and the other rare local minerals which have made the area famous. Call (973) 827-3481 for information. The museum is closed during January and February.

0.0 miles: Trail begins just north of Ogden Way.

0.1 miles: Adjacent to the trail is a cul-de-sac which runs off of Ogden Way. Here the trail detours slightly to avoid obstructions in the trail, then becomes eroded and steep before leveling off to its normal grade.

0.2 miles: The trail enters a cut as it begins an uphill climb.

0.3 miles: To the north and northwest, you can survey the once industrial valley which runs between Franklin and Ogdensburg. The trail continues uphill to the northeast.

0.5 miles: Up the hill you can see the remnants of a railbed which paralleled, then connected with this branch near a stone foundation a few hundred feet up the trail.

0.6 miles: Enter a deep cut through bedrock. Among the outcroppings is an artifact from the construction of the branch, a large piece of quarried rock which still exhibits drill marks and which actually has an old drill bit stuck in one of the holes.

0.7 miles: Leave the cut and pass over a filled section with a stream below.

1.1 miles: Pass under high voltage power lines. On a clear day, the High Point State monument is visible directly to the north. Trail jogs to the right slightly to bypass a missing culvert.

1.5 miles: Uphill from here is the still active mainline of the NYS&W.

1.7 miles: At this point the trail starts to enter a pass which intersects the Hamburg mountains. This historic pass is shared by the NYS&W mainline as well as by Route 23.

2.1 miles: To the right are a series of large stone piers which once supported elevated, open tracks. This area was used to off-load material such as coal from hopper cars on the mainline. The space below the elevated tracks and between the piers could store large quantities of coal or other materials for use by the locomotives on the main line and the Hanford branch. To the left are low concrete pillars which once supported a water tank for the locomotives.

2.6 miles: The trail ends next to the main line about 75 yards west of the Beaver Lake Road. Beaver Lake Junction was once a bustling area but today Route 23 is busy instead.

10 Henry Hudson Trail

Bay Shore Branch of Central New Jersey Railroad (CNJ)

Endpoints: Corner of Lloyd Road and Gerrard Avenue in Aberdeen
Township to North Leonard Avenue, Leonardo.
Location: Monmouth County, townships of Keyport, Union Beach,
Keansburg, Port Monmouth, Belford, and Leonardo.
Length: 9.0 miles
Surface: Asphalt
Maps: Keyport and Sandy Hook in the U.S.G.S. 1:24,000 series.
Uses: All non-motorized uses except horses.

To get there: Garden State Parkway to exit 117A. After paying the toll,
take a left at the "T" intersection. The trail parking lot is on the left just past
the next traffic light. A gas station is next to trail-head.

Contact:
Monmouth County Park System
805 Newman Springs Road, Lincroft, NJ 07738-1695   732-842-4000

Local Bed & Breakfast:
Hepburn House, 15 Monument St., Freehold, NJ 07728.   732-462-7696.
Seabird Inn, 60 Bay Ave., Highlands, NJ 07732.   732-872-0123.

Local resources for bike repair/rentals:
Atlantic Cyclery, 188 1st Ave, Atlantic Highlands, NJ 07716.
732-291-2664
Gallery 35 Bicycles, Route 35, Keyport, NJ 07735.   732-739-0978
Mike's Bikes, 46 First Ave., Atlantic Highlands, NJ 07716   732-291-8822

A charter was first granted in 1849 for a line from Freehold to Keyport, but
there was so much opposition that the charter expired. Another group got a
new charter in the 1860s and they began constructing a rail bed and track
from Freehold to Keyport. This was known as the Monmouth County
Agricultural Railroad (MCARR), and it opened for business around 1875.
About the same time, the Central Railroad of New Jersey (CNJ) developed
and opened the New York to Long Branch line. It crossed the MCARR
about 0.5 miles east of the Matawan station.

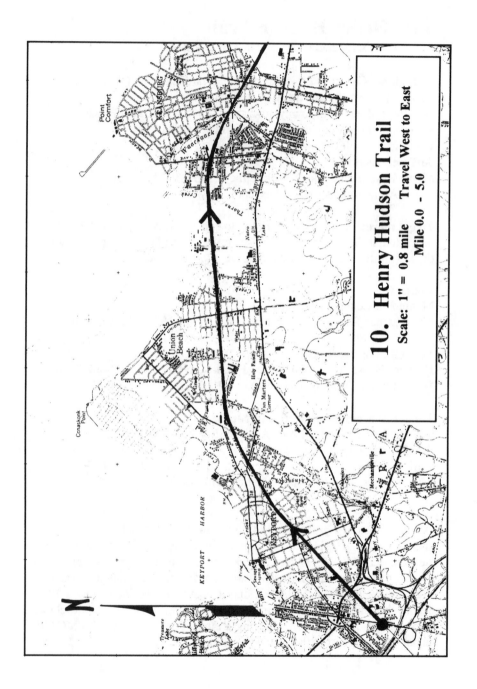

10. Henry Hudson Trail
Scale: 1" = 0.8 mile Travel West to East
Mile 0.0 - 5.0

There was a move by a group of merchants in Atlantic Highland to construct a line from that city through Hopping Station in Port Monmouth to Keyport. This later became known as the Bayshore Branch of the CNJRR, and it carried passengers until November 2, 1966. During its last stages it was carrying 400 passengers a day, 100 of which were pass-holders (people who were offered a free-pass). CNJ also provided freight service until around 1976 when Conrail took over service to the one remaining major customer, IFF Corporation in Union Beach. Conrail finally gave up the ghost in November of 1984.

Around 1984-85, the Freeholders (elected county officials) of Monmouth County floated a bond issue of approximately $5 million to purchase the 9-mile right-of-way from Conrail. The initial idea was to hold it for future development as a light-rail commuter serving the shore towns. But then the Bayshore economy was severely hurt by the economic recession of the late eighties and the attendant real estate collapse, and the plan for a commuter line was abandoned.

The property was then turned over to the Monmouth County Park Service (MCPS) to be developed as a recreational trail. Sections of it in Keyport had been used as a defacto trail, but most of the RoW was impassable, owing to the fact that 13 of the 14 bridges were out or unsafe. MCPS began to work on the trail around 1990, and finally dedicated it on July 4, 1995, as the Henry Hudson Trail. In 1997, MCPS purchased a structure in Atlantic Highlands, formerly the Snug Harbor restaurant. This enabled the rail-trail to be extended another 0.5 miles to Avenue D, Atlantic Highlands. The RoW from that point into town has been lost. However, the MCPS is negotiating to acquire a stretch of 3.5 miles along the shore, from the marina in Atlantic Highlands to Highlands borough. This would complete the rail-trail, following the path of a line that went to Highlands where it connected with a steam boat to New York. The original RoW is currently impassable and partly washed away.

0.0 miles: You will be starting at the corner of Gerard Avenue and Lloyd Road which has Fireman's Field nearby. Look for the old RR ties in the ditching on the right.
0.2 miles: Going past a cemetery on the left. Shortly thereafter, a slight fill will appear on the right. The bent timber bridge has pressure-treated decking with side railings that are about 4 feet high. This crosses a small stream called Luppatatong Creek.
0.3 miles: Crossing over the Garden State Parkway. Then you see Gateway Industrial Center, which shows signs of being rail-served at one time.

*Map of the New Jersey Central Railroad's Bayshore Branch, circa 1880
(From the collection of J. Wandres)*

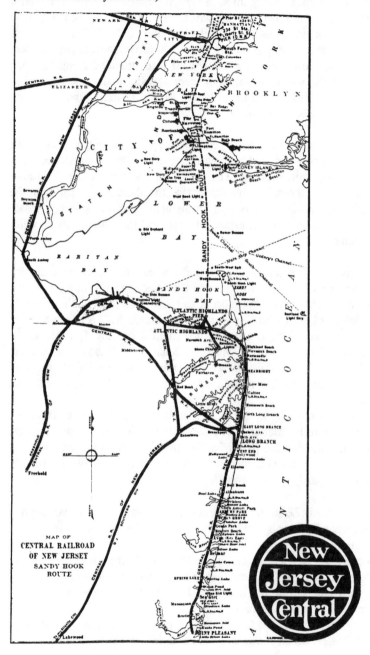

0.5 miles: Another industrial complex on the left was once rail served.

0.6 miles: Grade crossing of Beers Street and then into a tree-lined, canopied section that abuts houses.

0.8 miles: Grade crossing at Main Street and Hurley Street, with the Marie Curley ball field on the left.

0.9 miles: Grade crossing of Broad Street. The small fuel oil dealer here was most likely rail-served at one time.

1.1 miles: Grade crossing Church Street and Atlantic Avenue at an oblique angle, then back into the woods again with some backyards abutting again.

1.3 miles: Grade crossing at Green Grove Avenue near 5th Street. You can see a battery box here which has been recycled as a planter. Unusual width in this trail area suggests there was once a double track or small yard. There are ties still in place, as well as a telegraph signal pole with a catwalk.

1.5 miles: Grade crossing at Fulton Street is proceeded by a definite narrowing of the RoW.

1.6 miles: Electrical relay box with I-beam-shaped concrete footing. This is a typical Jersey Central construction standing about 5 feet high and badly rusted. Now crossing another bent timber bridge with 2 X 6 decking and side-rails. It crosses the Chingorora Creek. A telegraph signal is still here.

1.7 miles: Grade crossing at Stone Road. There is a battery box and signal case here, as well as another derelict signal pole with insulators.

2.0 miles: Grade crossing at Florence Avenue. Left side of trail has some modern houses. Jersey Power & Light has a truck facility in this area.

2.2 miles: Grade crossing of Poole Avenue at Morningside Avenue.

2.4 miles: Elementary School is at Wilson Street, followed by an area of tall marsh grasses. Crossing over another bent timber trestle similar to what you've seen before. Just after the bridge, a street will appear on the right. This is Jersey Avenue which was the site of a small station at one time. The area is wide-open around here and this suggests a possible team track site. A *Team Track* is a siding put in for general public access for car unloading or loading. This term refers to the team of horses which were used to pull the wagons and carts of cargo.

2.6 miles: Grade crossing at Spruce Street.

2.7 miles: Another one of the ubiquitous wooden bridges. This one crosses over Flat Creek.

2.9 miles: Grade crossing of Union Avenue.

3.1 miles: Crossing an inlet of the ocean by way of a bent timber bridge. On a clear day you can see the Manhattan skyline and the Varazaano Narrows Bridge. Next will be a grade crossing of the driveway for the IFF Corporation. Formerly known as NAPCO, this was the last customer on-line and quite possibly the reason the rail service lasted so long. This company makes a component used in the manufacture of perfume.

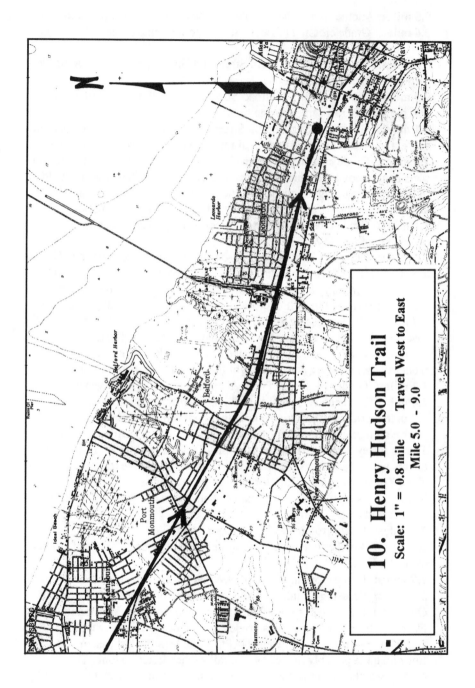

10. Henry Hudson Trail
Scale: 1" = 0.8 mile   Travel West to East
Mile 5.0 - 9.0

Bike trail-constructed bridge (non-railroad type) on the Henry Hudson Trail
(Photo by J. Wandres)

3.3 miles: A bike trail-constructed bridge (non-railroad type) with a little arch to it. This passes over some marshes and then onto a cinder fill/causeway to the mainland.

3.6 miles: A clearing appears with a gate, suggesting this was the rail route into the industrial complex.

3.7 miles: Another bent timber railroad bridge, then a marina on the left.

3.8 miles: Cul-de-sac appears, then more woods.

3.9 miles: Grade crossing of Central Avenue with 5th and 6th Avenues nearby.

4.2 miles: Grade Crossing of Laurel Avenue.

4.4 miles: This bridge is fairly long at about 100 feet and very similar to all the other railroad era bridges over the marshes. Coming up is another bit of hardwood forest and some residential apartments on the left.

4.5 miles: Grade crossing of Creek Road in Kearnesburg. There are stores here, as well as signs of a double-tracked right-of-way with a smattering of old rail-served industries still around. These include a building materials dealer and a metal fabrication shop.

5.3 miles: The area is wide here with concrete footings visible, giving evidence of railroad activity, and then an abrupt narrowing of the RoW. Access point is just across a small bridge. Deep woods on each side.

5.4 miles: Grade crossing at Atlantic Avenue.

5.6 miles: A ballfield is on the left and then a grade crossing at Thompson Avenue where the tracks are still in the road.

6.0 miles: Going over a corrugated steel culvert about 3 feet in diameter.

6.1 miles: Passing through a flood control dike.

6.2 miles: Back out in the marshes on another bent timber bridge. Interesting stubs of telegraph poles are observed here.

6.4 miles: Passing by more residential areas abutting just beyond tree line.

6.5 miles: Grade crossing at Bray Avenue. A large open area is here.

6.6 miles: Grade crossing at Main Street in Port Monmouth, with a water spigot still intact. The old railroad station is just ahead, along with a stationary caboose. Today they are part of a small park that is a goodwill area providing used clothing and other community services.

6.8 miles: Grade crossing at Wilson Avenue.

7.0 miles: On the approach to another one of the bent timber bridges.

7.1 miles: Grade crossing of Church Street at Railroad Avenue.

7.5 miles: Grade crossing of East Road.

8.5 miles: Passing by the driveway to the access point into the Earle Naval Weapons Station, and then under the Conrail bridge which carries the spur into the area.

8.8 miles: Grade crossing at Appleton Street.

8.9 miles: Grade crossing at Thompson Avenue at a traffic light.

9.0 miles: Grade crossing at North Leonard Avenue is the end of the trail.

Although similar to all other railroad era bridges over the marshes, this one on the Henry Hudson Trail is unusually long -- about 100 feet. (Photo by J. Wandres)

11 Kingston Branch Loop Trail

Kingston Branch of the Pennsylvania Railroad

Endpoints: South Brunswick township village of Kingston at Route 27 to the Georgetown Franklin Turnpike Route 518 at Rocky Hill in the township of Franklin.

Location: Somerset County, townships of Kingston and Rocky Hill.

Length: 3.7 miles

Surface: Stone-dust and gravel.

Map(s): Monmouth Junction and Rocky Hill in the 1:24,000 series, and Trenton in the 1:100,000 series.

Uses: Non-motorized uses except horses.

To get there: Start at the Princeton town line at the north end of Lake Carnegie. This trail-head is located at the intersection of the D & R Canal and Route 27. Plenty of opportunities for parking at either the John Fleemer Preserve , north side of Route 27 (donated by the Fleemer family in 1988 to the New Jersey Natural Lands Inc.), or at the smaller state parking lot on the south side of Route 27.

Contact:
Superintendent, D & R Canal State Park
625 Canal Road, Somerset, NJ 08873-7309.   732-873-3050

Local Bed & Breakfast:
Peacock Inn, 20 Bayard Lane, Princeton, NJ 08540.   609-924-1707

Local resources for bike repair:
Bike Shop at the Ski Barn, 29 Emmons Dr. Princeton, NJ 08540.
609-520-0222
Jay's Cycles, 249 Nassau St., Princeton, NJ 08540.   609-924-7233.
Kopp's Cycle, 38 Spring St., Princeton, NJ 08540.   609-924-1052

The linear nature of rail-trails does not usually lend itself to making loops or circuit routes such as those found in many hiking/bicycling guidebooks. But this Kingston Branch ride is unique and stands out from the others in this book because it travels a loop back to the starting point, using the rail corridor for the out-bound journey and then the canal tow-path for the return trip back. Though similar to the other leg of the D & R Canal which utilizes the Bel-Del Division (see Ride # 6), this trail ties into a different branch of the Pennsy, the Kingston Branch, and is part of the *East Coast Greenway* (see page 30). The trail description here follows the railroad side first (east side of canal), and then circles back on the canal tow-path.

11. Kingston Branch Loop Trail

Scale: 1" = 1.6 miles

At the Kingston trail-head is the Kingston Lock-Tender's house, now used by the Park personnel and interpreters. The elevation at Kingston is 56 feet above sea level, and the 24-foot wide and 220-foot long lock was used to raise or lower boats above seven feet in height. The Lock Tender's House was home to the employee and his family, and the small building nearby was his office. Local lore suggests that this operation was one of the earliest commercial installations of the Morse Telegraph in the United States.

Mule stables were once a part of the scene here at Kingston, where canal boat captains could hire a fresh team of mules. The railroad station was just across from the lock. You can visualize the RoW of the railroad since the rails are still in the street here and the brown fence line traces the line as it heads southeast towards Monmouth Junction and away from the canal.

0.0 miles: The trail starts at the Fleemer Preserve on the north side of Route 27.

0.1 miles: The trail starts out with a trap rock surface which then turns into fine stone dust in about 50 yards or so. An underground oil pipeline shares the corridor with you for part of the way. (Besides being a great opportunity for recreation and heritage or eco-tourism, Rail-Trails are also a great place to install pipelines or fiber optic networks.) There is also in this initial area an old drain weir for the canal. A *Weir* is usually built of stone or masonry and is a safety valve that prevents the canal from overflowing and sustaining damage.

0.4 miles: A bog on the right allows water to pass through to the canal by way of some three-foot cast-iron culverts. Many ties are seen here, slowly rotting away into the landscape.

1.3 miles: Just becoming visible on the right is the big quarry of the Trap Rock Industries, Inc. (TRI). This quarry was the last rail-served customer of the railroad and one of the main reasons why the railroad even came here in the first place. The hillside where TRI operates is the location where George Washington wrote his most famous speech, *The Farewell to the Troops*. The house in which he was staying and writing used to stand where the big aggregate operation is now. This house was preserved and moved to another location, but the land has been utilized for its mineral resources.

1.9 miles: This marks the end of the out-bound journey of the loop via the rail corridor. Trail-head parking and restrooms are here at the north end of the trail at the Georgetown Franklin Turnpike. Before taking the canal tow-path for your return trip back, you might like to investigate the historical surroundings, beginning with visiting the kiosk that describes some of the quarry history.

The quarry began in the 1860s and the trap rock was used to pave the streets of Jersey City and Newark. Excavation has been continuous since then. In Griggstown, just north of here, a copper mine was established in the late 1700s. The RoW in this immediate area was donated to the people of New Jersey by the TRI Company to create the trail.

The foundation seen here is the Rocky Hill bridge tender's house. It was erected by the canal company to house the employee responsible for the raising and lowering of the bridge to allow water borne traffic to continue on the canal. Until 1926, every bridge on the canal had a bridge tender's house alongside to ensure there would be someone to raise the bridge at all times, including night operations. Such houses still standing along the canal can be found at Griggstown, Blackwell's Mills, and East Millstone.

The village of Rocky Hill at the north end of the trail is an interesting place. It began in the mid 1700s with the construction of saw and grist mills along the Millstone River. Very little development occurred until the mid 1800s. Growth was boosted by the construction of the canal in 1834 and the spur of the Camden & Amboy Railroad in 1864 (later to be called the Kingston Branch of the Pennsylvania Railroad). By the end of the 1800s, business along the railroad and the canal began to decline, followed by the failure of many of the local businesses that were geared to the canal or the railroad. By the early 1900s, Rocky Hill changed its focus and moved most of the town's buildings and businesses up the hill. Visiting the town today, you will see that it looks much like it did in 1900. The Atlantic Terra Cotta Company was another major employer in the area, established in the late 1800s as a manufacturer of decorative tiles for buildings. Some of the more prominent locations were the Woolworth Building in New York and the Philadelphia Museum of Art.

1.9 miles: This is the turn for the return trip. Cross over the canal by way of the wooden automobile bridge and then head back on the tow-path side of the canal. Viewed from this side, you can now have a good view of the flag stones that provide the containment for the canal with the Millstone River.
2.4 miles: Concrete mile-marker here dates back to the canal operations era and says "21 Miles" towards Bordentown; the other side says "23 Miles" to New Brunswick. Here you are nearly at the half way point of the canal.
2.7 miles: A dam is seen on the Millstone River.
3.4 miles: Concrete mile-marker (twin to the last one) noting "20 Miles" to Bordentown and "24 Miles" to New Brunswick.
3.7 miles: At the start point again. You will note though that a tunnel is under the road, allowing for safe passage of bikes and pedestrians under the busy Route 27. You can continue to Princeton and beyond to Trenton by following the tow-path west.

This sign, located at the start of the Kingston Branch Loop Trail, is from about 1930

12 Linwood Bikeway
Somers Point Branch of the Pennsylvania-Reading Seashore Lines Railroad (PRSL)

Endpoints: Oak Crest Avenue, Linwood, to Bethel Road, Somers Point
Location: Atlantic County, cities of Linwood and Somers Point
Length: 3.0 miles
Surface: Asphalt
Map(s): Atlantic City, U.S.G.S. 1:24,000 series
Uses: Non-motorized uses, except horses.

To get there: Take Garden State Parkway to exit 36 to County Route 563. Follow this south about 1.5 miles to Wabash Avenue. Take this 7 blocks south to the intersection of Oak Crest Avenue. This is the border with the community of Northfield. The trail-heads south from here.

Contact:
Gary Gardener, City Clerk, Linwood City Hall
400 Poplar Avenue, Linwood NJ 08221. 609-927-4108

Local Bed & Breakfast:
White Manor Inn, 739 S 2nd Avenue, Absecon, NJ 08201. 609-748-3996

Local resources for bike repairs:
Village Schwinn Shop, 606 New Rd., Somers Point, NJ 08244.
609-927-3775

This line, built in 1880, became the Shore Fast Line which originated in Atlantic City and headed south through Pleasantville to Somers Point and then out on a causeway to Ocean City. It became electrified in 1906, running orange trolley cars that were known locally for their on-time service. The inter-urban service ran until 1948. Freight service continued on to Somers Point, but freight service to Ocean City ran through the Tuckahoe Branch (See Ride # 15). By the mid-1960s, the Somers Point Branch was only seeing bi-weekly service, so it came to an end in 1966.

This trail is different from all the others in this book because of the layout of the RoW. The trail is paved, 10 feet wide, and is in the grassy area between two parallel streets that have suburban/urban single family houses between them. There are many streets to note and cross on this trail, but the majority are neighborhood streets and don't present a great safety problem. A sign at the north end of the trail says *Welcome to Linwood's George K. Francis Bikeway*.

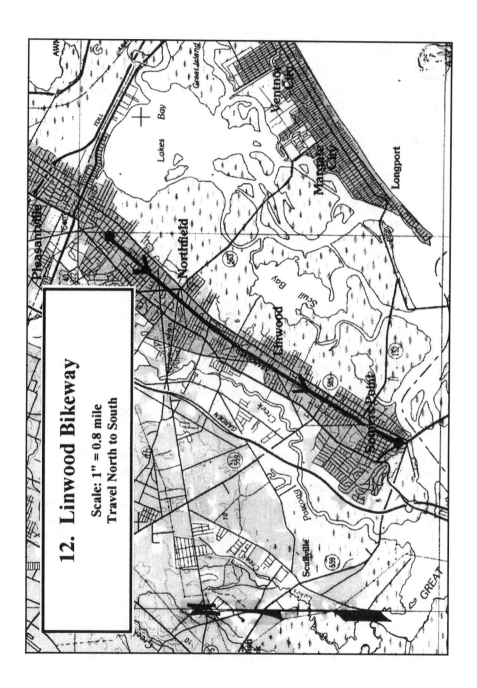

12. Linwood Bikeway

Scale: 1" = 0.8 mile
Travel North to South

98

0.0 miles: Starting at Oak Crest.

0.8 miles: Poplar and Wabash Streets are where the Linwood Passenger station can still be found, albeit as a well-done replica. The Linwood Market, an old fashioned, good-service market, is across the street and has been in business since 1901.

1.0 miles: A ball field is on the left. Here at Tabor Avenue, the city has provided many parking spaces for trail users. A regional high school is nearby and more schools are just ahead.

2.2 miles: Going past Patcong Avenue.

3.0 miles: Hartshorne Park is here and the trail ends at Bethel Road, near Center Street in the community of Somers Point.

A well-built replica of the Linwood Passenger Station, located on the Linwood Bikeway

13 Middlesex Greenway
Lehigh Valley Railroad's Perth Amboy Branch

Endpoints: Middlesex Avenue in Metuchen to Crows Mill Road in the village of Fords
Location: Middlesex County, town of Metuchen
Length: 3.8 miles
Surface: Cinder and gravel
Map(s): Perth Amboy, U.S.G.S. 1:24,000 series
Uses: Non-motorized uses, except horses

To get there:
From Route 287 North: take exit 2A to Route 27 North. Follow this about 0.5 miles to Lake Avenue. Memorial Park is on the left. Turn left onto Memorial Parkway.
From Route 287 South: take Exit 3 marked Metuchen-New Durham Road. Keep left on the ramp and turn left at bottom of ramp onto New Durham Road and follow this into Metuchen. When it bends to the left, it becomes Middlesex Avenue. At Lake Avenue, also called Route 27, turn right. After the next traffic light, you will go over a bridge above the Greenway. Immediately after the bridge, turn right onto the Memorial Parkway where you will find parking spaces.

Contact:
Bob Takash, Edison Greenways Group
P.O. Box 10432, New Brunswick, NJ 08906. 732-985-5821

Local Lodging:
Sheraton-Edison, Raritan Center Parkway, Edison, NJ 08877.
732-225-8300
Ramada Inn ,Woodbridge Avenue, Edison NJ 08877. 800-272-6232

Local resources for bike repair:
Bike N Gear, 531 Old Post Road, Edison, NJ 08817. 732-287-6996.
Metuchen Bicycle Sales & Service, 457 Main Street, Metuchen, NJ 08840.
732-548-1954

In the book *Boyhood Days of Old Metuchen*, author David Trumbull-Marshall tells of the construction of the railroad which was planned to go through the Marshall house on Amboy Avenue, forcing the family to move.

One day a party of surveyors drove down stakes on our property. I and my younger brother...pulled up the stakes because we did not want any railroad running through our house. The next day the surveyors came back and threatened me and my brother with dire punishment if we pulled up any more stakes, and to add force to their threats, actually began to hack at the corner of our house with a hatchet.

This railroad, the first to go through the Metuchen and Edison area, was the Pennsylvania Railroad and now it is AMTRAK's Northeast Corridor. The other railroad line through town was the Lehigh Valley Railroad (LV). The LV was built in the 1870s primarily to take the coal from the mines of eastern Pennsylvania to both the Great Lakes terminal at Buffalo and the New York City market at Jersey City. At the Great Lakes, the LV and some competing railroads even maintained a fleet of ships that carried the black gold to the Midwest. These maritime operations were shut down by the Interstate Commerce Commission around the time of the first World War. The federal government felt the monopolistic tendencies of these water operations exacerbated the threat that the railroad companies might take over the traffic from the conventional steam ship companies.

Locally, the Lehigh Valley Railroad maintained a large yard in South Plainfield where some of the coal was destined to be sent east on a secondary line through Metuchen and Edison, to the Perth Amboy coal docks which date back to 1873. The remnants of this terminal operation can be seen in Perth Amboy along the Arthur Kill, south of the Outer Bridge Crossing.

The Lehigh Valley RR lived and died with the coal market. For example, in 1948, coal represented over 40% of their car-load traffic. At this time, coal was the preferred fuel for homes and was the important ingredient of the so-called smoke-stack industries. By 1960, with the changeover in the home heating market to gas and fuel oil, this figure dropped to under 20%. The situation was so bad on the single commodity-dependent LV that in 1962, the Pennsylvania Railroad was allowed to take control and try to facilitate a rescue, but the downward slide continued anyway.

With the creation of Conrail in 1976, the line saw service, but not much in the way of upgrades or creative marketing initiatives, and it continued to decline until Conrail finally abandoned the line in 1986. The idea of a Greenway germinated in the fall of 1990 in Metuchen, promoted by Mayor John Wiley. Conrail finally pulled out the rails and ties in November of 1993.

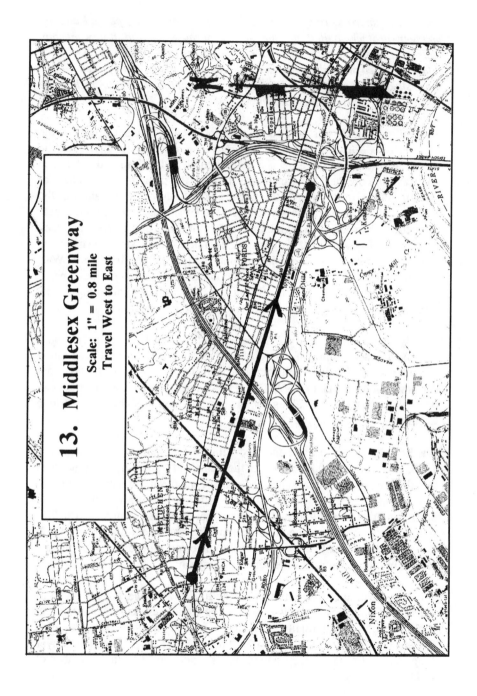

13. Middlesex Greenway

Scale: 1" = 0.8 mile
Travel West to East

0.0 miles: Grade crossing at Middlesex Avenue. This is the beginning of the trail. The Oakite Company complex across the street was the last rail-served customer in the area. Now closed and for sale, it is a forlorn statement of the long-gone industrial age. Also across the street, a branch came off the LV to connect to the Pennsy. This connection gave the LV a passenger connection to New York City. The line was carried over Middlesex Avenue where the abutments still stand and an alignment can be seen through the wooded area just north of the trail RoW. Just to the left or south before Middlesex Avenue is a large open field where Freeman's Lumberyard used to stand until it burned in the 1940s.

0.1 miles: The AMTRAK Northeast Corridor mainline crosses overhead. The concrete bridge, built in 1914, today carries four tracks and sees numerous trains each day. As the trail curves to the north slightly, a battery box for signals can be seen.

0.2 miles: Just beyond the tree line to the south is Memorial Park. Look for the concrete slab with angle-braced, wooden 3 X 8s supporting a wooden 4 X 10 that has been sawed-off. This structure was most likely a tell-tale signal. A *Tell-tale* was a series of wires or ropes that hung down over the tracks from a cross-arm. They would brush against the back of anyone on top of the cars, thus warning of a dangerous object ahead with restricted overhead clearance, like a bridge or tunnel. You are heading into a cut now that will become steadily deeper.

0.3-0.5 miles: The cut has grown to over 20 feet tall, and with the canopy of trees overhead, the trail will be 10-12 degrees cooler here than the street level in the summer. When the line here was built in 1873, the major digging was done by Italian and Irish immigrants with pick axes and shovels, loading the excavation into carts to haul it away. When they ran into bedrock, they employed the newly invented nitroglycerin.

Three bridges are seen in this section. The first or westernmost bridge carries Route 27. Near the northeast side of the bridge is the remains of the concrete footing for the Metuchen Station at Lake Avenue. The Lehigh Valley's Metuchen station was up the slope and was accessed by a wooden staircase. There was a provision in the narrow cut for double tracks, and the station was torn down during World War II. A bunk house for railroad employees was also near here. Looking at the south abutment, you'll see a U.S. Government Geodetic Survey marker that was installed in 1942.

The middle span is the Graham Avenue Bridge. Out of service for many years to both vehicular traffic and pedestrians, it is scheduled to be demolished in 1998 by NJ DOT. There is funding to build a generic concrete automobile bridge, but nothing is available yet to build a pedestrian bridge that just might reconnect the neighborhood in a sustainable and livable way. There is a talk of doing a pedestrian bridge here, but no action is imminent. The house on the right nearest the bridge was owned by Governor George Silzer, a governor of New Jersey from 1923-1926.

The eastern-most bridge carries Main Street, which leads to the nearby NJ Transit Station and a beautifully restored downtown Metuchen. Note the turn-of-the-century wooden drain trough carrying rain water from Main Street to the RoW's drainage ditches. It's amazing to see such a structure still intact and in service. This is also the break point for the drainage system. Some might call it the continental divide for eastern New Jersey. (According to the *Environmental Resources Inventory*, Metuchen, NJ, 1976, west flowing water goes to the Dismal Brook to Bound Brook to Green Brook to the Raritan River. The east flowing water goes to Mill Brook and then into the Raritan River.)

0.8 miles: The local Mosquito Commission has been working here to improve the flow of the drainage ditches. Look for the few stray rails left behind, including one that is about 60 lb. Such thin rail was meant for extremely light duty, such as a trolley line. Perhaps this is a remnant of the Elizabethtown & Trenton Trolley Line (E & T Trolley).

0.9 miles: A paper converting company known as Graphic Equipment Corporation is on the north side of the trail. On the left are some apartment buildings on Green Street with an access point for the Greenway.

1.0 miles: Concrete culvert with its out-fall on the south side.

1.2 miles: In this area stood the Pierson Avenue Bridge, which was one of those old spindly wooden structures that had approaches that were so steep, you couldn't see the other side of the bridge. It was torn down in 1997 and replaced with the modern generic guard-railed culvert that allows for no trail passage. The trail approaches up to Pierson Avenue are gentle though, and there are many restaurants, stores, banks and a mall (Tano Mall) in the area. Pierson Avenue is the border between Metuchen and Edison.

1.3 miles: A possible side trail may spur off to the north in this area leading to the Tano Mall. This new spur trail would utilize the electric utility RoW which formally used to be the Elizabethtown & Trenton Trolley Line. The line was also known as the Public Service Fast Line Trolley system. Note the still visible old abutments for this trolley line. Route 1 is above you, and just on the west side is an old culvert built by the railroad.

1.4 miles: The Public Service Electric & Gas Training Center and electric substation is on the right. This utility has been an important supporter of the trail. Note the old siding leading into complex. There used to be a large coal fired plant and the isolated siding here fed coal to the plant.

1.5 miles: Just beyond is the Jackson Avenue grade crossing and the large open area was an industrial complex called Richmond Radiator Company that burned down in 1995. They made ceramic components.

Years ago, there were many ceramics refractories making the knob & tube components for the old-style electric wiring. They were taking advantage of the abundant clay found nearby. Thomas Edison's lab in Menlo Park was nearby, and many ancillary electrical supply businesses sprang up around him. This area was once called the Phoenix neighborhood of Edison. And today, like a Phoenix, the neighborhood is literally rising from the ashes of the days of the smokestack industries. On the left will be access to the ball fields which are part of the Herbert Hoover Middle School. Note the triple arm telegraph poles still standing, though no insulators are intact.

1.8-2.0 miles: A grade crossing here at Liddle Avenue still has the large, ancient, cross-buck sign warning of the train. Evidence exists in this area that the railroad used to be double track, and then in the last years of operation it became single tracked. Zestron, a Johns Manville Company, is on the south side of the trail. They used to have a three car siding and were a constant customer of the railroad. They are still in business today, manufacturing some PVC products. You are now on the approach to the bridge carrying the New Jersey Turnpike over the trail. This huge 12-lane highway overpass is much like a tunnel. It should also be noted that both natural gas and petroleum pipelines cross underneath the trail in this area.

2.1 miles: You are now passing through a fairly wide open area. The fenced off area to the south was at one time Seaboard Refractories, another of the local clay industries. During World War II, a spur came off of here, connecting into the Raritan Arsenal. In more recent years there has been talk of making the site a six hotel complex. A little stream through here may have some woodchucks and other wildlife visible.

2.3 miles: Grade crossing at Woodbridge Avenue. This is a dangerous crossing because of the limited sight lines and speed of the cars. You probably should head left to the next street corner and use the stop light to cross over to the other side. Before you head off though, take note of the 1940s-era grade crossing standard. It's not too often that you can see such a bit of antiquity on the streets of today. The large relay box is also a rather archaic device. Just across the street is the gold dome of the St. Nicholas Church. The modern complex known as the Edison Corporate Center is sited above the remains of another long-gone clay company.

2.4 miles: Visible on the right is a set of steps installed by an abutter who wants easy access to the trail. Obviously he's a very handy guy because in addition to the stairs, he also has built many bird-houses.

2.5 miles: Heading west, you are now going through the Clara Barton section of town, named of course for the Civil War nurse who later formed the Red Cross. Check out the signal box for grade crossing signals. This will be on the right and stands about 8 feet tall and is mounted on concrete posts. The right-of-way in this area is very much open and was at one time double tracked.

2.6 miles: The trail is still fairly wide open since the RoW is 100 feet wide. A stream is accompanying you on the north side of the trail. Houses on the left are on dead-end streets that abut the trail. You are now going into a bit of a cut that is about 12 feet deep.

2.8 miles: King George Post Road is passing overhead now by way of a modern concrete bridge. In the 1980s, this structure replaced an old wooden one. This was originally a colonial road from New York to Philadelphia via New Brunswick and Trenton. The industrial complex known as the Fords Terminal Warehouse Company, which used to store special industrial ceramics, is on the right as you enter the Fords section of Edison. You are then heading uphill and out of the cut as the neighborhood houses continue on the left. An old lumber yard known as Fords Lumber used to be here as well.

3.1-3.5 miles: A fill is building through here as the ground starts to drop away to the right. This was the site of an old claypit. The height will afford you a view of Route 440 and the surrounding areas. A modern apartment complex on the right is a neighbor to the trail.

3.6 miles: Passing under Crows Mills Road. Raritan Center Industrial Park is on the right as you are now near where the junction is made to the active track that leads to the industrial park. Raritan Center Industrial Park is about 1.5 miles from the junction.

3.8 miles: A forgotten and abandoned track is adjacent to you now on the left. The rail dates back to 1925 and is 115 lb. (The weight of rail is expressed in pounds per three foot section. Modern high-speed rail is around 135-150 lb., while trolley or other light-rail is under 60 lbs.) The tie plates and ties are also still in place. Note the small 6 X 8 concrete footing on the ground where the railroad came through. This was most likely a coal transloading chute which led to the industrial complex. East William Street Park is adjacent in this area and can provide parking for trail users. The trail ends before the junction with the semi-active rail ahead.

What is an Orphan Bridge?

There were three bridges over the Greenway corridor that were known as orphan bridges. Why the term *orphan bridge*? When Conrail was created in the mid 1970s, they did not acquire the bridges over the corridor. Since the bridges were not a part of Conrail holdings, the term *orphan bridge* came into being. In the late 1980s, the State of New Jersey set up a trust fund for the removal and repair of orphan bridges. Since then, the NJ Department of Transportation (DOT) has been working on a plan to remove the Graham Avenue bridge in Metuchen, repair the Main Street bridge in Metuchen, and remove the Pierson Avenue bridge in Edison.

---

14 Monroe Township Bikeway
Williamstown Branch of the Pennsylvania-Reading Seashore Lines (PRSL)

Endpoints: Church St. and Bodine Avenue in Williamstown to Fries Road
Location: Gloucester County, town of Williamstown
Length: 3.5 miles
Surface: Paved and gravel
Map(s): Williamstown and Pitman East in the U.S.G.S. 1:24,000 series, and the Hammontown and Wilmington in the 1:100,000 series.
Uses: Non-motorized uses. Horses not allowed on the paved section within the town of Williamstown

To get there: The town of Willamstown is located at the intersection of Route 322 and Route 42, and south of exit 38 off the Atlantic City Express Way. Go to Church Street, which is south of Route 322, and park at the ballfield on the corner of Bodine Ave.

Contact:
Deborah Terch, Community Affairs Director
Monroe Township Dept. of Parks and Recreation
301 Bluebell Rd, Williamstown, NJ 08094. 609-728-9823

Local Bed & Breakfast:
Victorian Rose Farm B & B, 947 Route 40, Woodstown, NJ 08098.
609-769-4600

Local resources for bike repair:
Bikeline, 1809 N Black Horse Pike, Williamstown NJ 08094.
609-875-1910

The Pennsylvania-Reading Seashore Lines (PRSL) was one of those rare railroads that held a special place in the hearts of those in the communities they served. The company was forged from a union of two competing companies that jointly decided to merge together and fight the true competition, trucks, rather than continue fighting each other. It all began when both the Reading Railroad and the Pennsylvania Railroad were laying track together to reach the resort of Atlantic City in 1880. Both companies then turned south to lay track and build to the resorts of Ocean City, Wildwood, and Cape May. As the tourist traffic to the Jersey shore grew in value, each railroad continually tried to out-do the other -- price wars, faster trains, better service, etc., etc.

By the 1920s, busses and cars began to gain importance in transportation, and the two railroads saw the handwriting on the wall. They started negotiations to combine operations and on June 25, 1933, the deal was sealed with all the necessary local and state approvals. Thus creating the PRSL, with Pennsy having 2/3 control, they immediately set out to consolidate and remove duplicate trackage and facilities. The railroad was undergoing a transformation because even though the passenger traffic was succumbing to cars, the freight business was growing with the industrial expansion in South Jersey.

The line was merged into the Penn-Central disaster in 1968. When both PC and Reading went bankrupt in 1972, the PRSL became part of Conrail. Today many of these branch lines are abandoned, though a few operate successfully as shortlines, independent of Conrail. Much of the RoW of these old Reading and Pennsy lines have been obliterated and lost forever. Here, however, is an interesting and enjoyable piece of South Jersey history.

0.0 miles: Starting at the park which has ample parking and restrooms, head east (left.)

0.2 miles: The start of the trail begins at the corner of Church Street and Railroad Avenue. The trail is about 10 feet wide and has a sewer line underneath. Shortly ahead is a grade crossing of Chestnut Street near Marion Avenue, then the trail bends left with residential houses on each side.

0.6 miles: Trail ends at Route 322 where the Police station sits. There is a convenience store here, but not much public parking. The line used to continue northeast from here, all the way to a place named Williamstown Junction, which came off the main and led directly to Williamstown. This was located between Camden and Winslow, and it was abandoned in 1934. The section that continued northeast from Williamstown Junction to Atco was abandoned in 1942.

Turn around now and head back to the starting point.

0.2 miles: Parallel to the trail on the left is the Don Pattino Pizza Sauce and Violet Packing Company. A railroad siding is still here and in the fenced in area is a truck scale. It is unclear what the former use was. Residential housing is on the right, and you come upon Clayton Road where you will cross at grade. Check out the power substation along the trail after Clayton Road. It is not like your typical ones being built of brick and mortar; this is built to last.

0.7 miles: Going past a number of schools and ball fields as the trail is numbered with mileage markers. A housing development is on the right.

0.9 miles: Lightly forested, and then more schools and houses as the forest disappears.

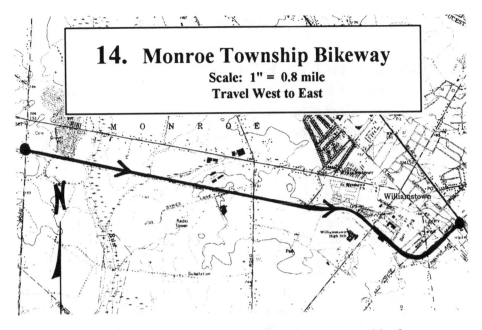

14. Monroe Township Bikeway

Scale: 1" = 0.8 mile

Travel West to East

1.2 miles: You are now back into more woods with a power corridor for company.

1.5 miles: End of the paved trail at County Route 522. Many years ago, there used to be flag stop station here which was called Robanna. Follow the trail across the street and onto the gravel section of the trail.

1.7 miles: Grade crossing of Sykes Lane. Note the cinder mixed in the dirt.

1.9 miles: A quarry is seen here. Being so close to Glassboro, it is not surprising to run into this. Glassboro was a bevy of activity for the glass industry for many years, and this is one of the many sand quarries in the area that fed the maw of the glass industry. This is a fairly large open area and the railroad RoW is above the quarry area. You'll probably see some ATVs in this area.

2.4 miles: A twin culvert is seen here. The modern, corrugated steel one is obviously the secondary one. The much older iron one is the primary.

2.9 miles: Two more culverts in the area allow a stream called the Scotland Run to pass from north to south. These culverts are fairly large at 7 feet in diameter.

3.0 miles: In the midst of a brand new development containing many 3,000-square-foot houses.

3.3 miles: You are now passing through an apple orchard.

3.5 miles: Grade crossing at Fries Mills Road and the site of the former station called Downer. This is the effective end of the trail as the RoW has been purchased by the abutters. There is an interesting gift shop across the street from the end of the trail, the Herrmann Landscaping and Gift Shop.

15 Ocean City Branch

Ocean City Branch of the Pennsylvania-Reading Seashore Lines Railroad (PRSL)

Endpoints: Within the city of Ocean City
Location: Cape May County, Ocean City
Length: 25 blocks
Surface: Asphalt
Map(s): Ocean City, U.S.G.S. 1:24,000 series
Uses: All non-motorized uses, except horses.

To get there: Take the Garden State Parkway to Exit 29, then Route 9
north to County Route 52 to Ocean City. Once you are into Ocean City
itself, take the 5th right onto Haven Avenue. Park near the Transportation
Center which is the old PRSL Passenger Station.

Contact:
George Savastano, Ocean City DPW
1040 Haven Avenue, Ocean City NJ 08226. 609-399-6111

Local Bed & Breakfast:
New Brighton Inn B & B, 519 5th Street, Ocean City, 08226. 609-399-2829
Ocean Breeze Guest House, 1234 Ocean Avenue, Ocean City, NJ 08226.
609-399-7248
Scarborough Inn, 720 Ocean Avenue, Ocean City, NJ 08226.
609-399-1558
Serendipity B & B, 712 9th Street, Ocean City, NJ 08826. 800-842-8544
Northwood Inn B & B, 401 Wesley Avenue, Ocean City, NJ 08826.
609-399-6071
Castle By the Sea, 701 Ocean Avenue, Ocean City, NJ 08226.
609-398-3555

Local sources for bike repair/rentals:
Annarelli's Bicycle Store, 1014 Asbury Avenue, Ocean City, NJ 08226.
609-399-2238
Cal's, 1706 Asbury Avenue, Ocean City, NJ 08226. 609-399-1623

The City of Ocean City has an interesting history. It was founded in 1879,
when three Methodist ministers established it as an alcohol-free and family
oriented resort. It grew so fast that it became a city in 1897, though wholly
owned by the legal arm of the Methodists, the Ocean City Association. This
type of arrangement was not uncommon; similar arrangements were taking
place in Willimantic, Connecticut, and in Northampton and Oak Bluffs,
Massachusetts, as well as in Round Lake, New York.

The Ocean City community was eager to become an easy way to get to heaven-on-earth for the good Christian families it hoped to attract, so the town fathers met with some railroad companies to have them build a line into the Ocean City. The West Jersey and Seashore Railroad was attracted to build to the shore by the town's offer to (1) secure all easements and titles for the RoW; (2) grade and otherwise prepare that corridor; (3) provide land for a station. -- All for free! All the railroad had to do was to lay track and run the trains. Accordingly, the trains started running in November of 1884. This original line into town ran down the middle of West Avenue.

A competing line, the South Jersey Railroad, came to town by way of Tuckahoe in 1898. This dual railroad build-out paralleled much of South Jersey. The South Jersey Railroad was controlled by the Reading Railroad and the original line was a subsidiary of the Pennsylvania Railroad.

The railroads brought out the tourists by the thousands because apparently, people were starved for a family-oriented resort -- a place where the sun and surf were the draw, not the honky-tonk bars that populated the other towns of the Jersey Shore.

Both the Reading and the Pennsylvania Railroads competed through their subsidiaries for the tourist traffic to the shore and built many duplicate routes. The barrier islands along the Jersey shore were particularly suited for developing resort communities. Both railroads built mainlines along the mainland shoreline and then built causeways across the marshes to get to the communities out onto the barrier islands.

The competing railroads saw the folly of continuing to fight one another when they realized their real competition were the private automobiles, buses, and trolley. (Yes, Ocean City once had a trolley with connections to Atlantic City by way of a causeway of timbers across the bay. It was abandoned during World War II and the causeway was torn out in 1946.) The two formerly competing lines were merged into one corporation on June 25, 1933, called the Pennsylvania-Reading Seashore Lines.

With the consolidation of the railroads, the line in West Avenue was torn out and only the Haven Avenue corridor stayed active. Once West Avenue was reconstructed as a wide thoroughfare for automobiles, the land adjacent to the street became part of a small real estate boom which resulted in the building of many of the structures you see today on West Avenue.

In the 1950s, the stations at North Street and 4th Avenue were shuttered and the end of the line was at 10th Avenue. By this time the full passenger train was replaced with a single, self-powered Buddliner Rail Diesel Car, (RDC). Since the railroad had to contend with seasonal traffic only, occasional flooding at inopportune times, and the coming of the automobile, only the PRSL routes into Wildwood, Ocean City, and Cape May were still intact by the early 1950s. Today, though virtually fully developed and densely populated, Ocean City still shows its early influences and is more family oriented than the sister communities along the Jersey Shore.

Since this trail is so short, a guide based on mileage is not practical. Instead, the ride description uses the well-marked and easy-to-follow street signs. Ocean City is divided into a dense grid-like network of streets that are marked 1st Street (northernmost) through 59th Street (southernmost). These number streets run east-west for the entire length of the community. The trail in this community follows either directly on just next to Haven Avenue, from 10th Street to 35th Street.

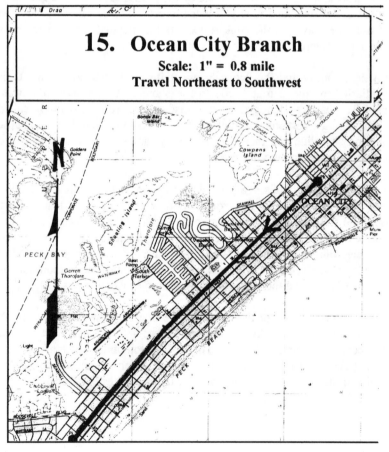

15. Ocean City Branch
Scale: 1" = 0.8 mile
Travel Northeast to Southwest

10th Street: The Passenger Station of the old PRSL RR stands here and has been converted to a bus terminal. The structure itself is in good condition and is of typical hip-roofed construction. Haven Avenue is actually the route of the train, and the track used to be (and in some small sections still is) in the street. Head south along Haven Avenue.

15th - 16th Street: Peter Lumber Company is here. This is an old style, friendly-service, neighborhood type operation that is not seen so often anymore. This still viable business was one of the last rail-served customers in town, and the freight storage sheds with rail-door openings are still here.

20th Street: Track is still in the street here.

24th Street: The RoW is now gone, so take a left at 25th Street and go right on West Avenue. Go four blocks and then turn right onto 29th Street.

34th -35th Street:. Here the trail is set right down the middle of Haven Avenue and is dressed-up with interesting plantings. The bike path ends at 35th Street.

*Antique brochure
published by the
Shore Fast Line
(Author's collection)*

**A Sixteen Mile Ride Over
the "Shore Fast Line's" Famous Scenic
Route to Ocean City**

One Day Round Trip Excursion 75¢

Fifty minutes spent in comfortable High Speed Electric cars carry you over the interesting meadowland through the charming communities of Pleasantville, Northfield, Linwood and Somers Point, riding for many miles thru the invigorating pines; then over Great Egg Harbor Bay into the water resort of Ocean City with its two and one-half miles of Boardwalk lined with attractive shops, a beautiful bathing beach and hotels modern in every respect. Take cars at Virginia Ave. and Boardwalk, Atlantic City and at all street intersections on Atlantic Ave. between Virginia Ave. and Mississippi Ave.

Every 30 Minutes
On the Hour and Half Hour

*See all and do all
by the* »»SHORE FAST LINE

16 Ogden Mine Railroad Path

Edison Branch of the Central New Jersey Railroad (CNJ)

Endpoints: Hurdtown within the borders of the Mahlon Dickerson Reservation
Location: Morris and Sussex Counties, towns of Hurdtown and Sparta
Length: 2.4 miles
Surface: Original ballast and cinder
Map(s): Franklin, U.S.G.S 1:24,000 series
Uses: All non-motorized uses.

To get there: Take I-80 to Exit 34B for Sparta. Follow State Route 15 north towards the Picatinny Arsenal. Take Route 15 for five miles to a clearly marked interchange for Weldon Road, on the right. Take Weldon Road for about three miles on a gravel surface. This trail has no parking at either end, although it can be accessed by cyclists. It is easiest to park at the Saffins Pond parking lot and then travel in either direction along the trail. There are many other trails in the park, some of which form loops with the rail trail. The official county map of the park is useful, so be sure to call or write for a copy.

Contact:
Morris County Park Commission
P.O. Box 1295, Morristown, NJ 07962-1295. 973-326-7600

Local Lodging:
Westin-Morristown Hotel, 2 Whipanny Rd., Morristown, NJ 07960.
973-539-7300
Madison Hotel, 1 Convent Road, Morristown, NJ 07960. 973-285-1800

Local resources for bike repair/rentals:
Marty's Reliable Cycle of Morristown, 173 Speedwell Avenue, Morristown, NJ 07960. 973-538-7773

Part of the following information is from a brochure published by the New Jersey RailTrails, a state-wide non-profit group that works to turn abandoned railroads into multi-use public trails. Information about joining is available by writing to P.O. Box 23, Pluckemin, NJ 07978, or by calling 215-340-9974.

This rail line was a continuation of the one described in Ride # 1 (Berkshire Valley WMA Trail). In 1855, five iron and other mineral mines were active around what is now Mahlon Dickerson Reservation, including the upper and lower Weldon Mines located near the existing water treatment building. The Ogden Mine Railroad (OMRR) was originally built to service these and other mines. The OMRR was originally built in 1864 and connected to the outside world by way of a water borne connection at Lake Hopatcong where canal boats took the ore to the furnaces. Before the days of cheap transportation, iron ore was smelted to metallic iron in small blast furnaces, close to the mines. These furnaces used charcoal made from local forests and water power from the nearby streams. Eventually, when the forests were laid bare and charcoal became scarce, the larger and more efficient blast furnaces based on anthracite coal came into use.

This line never had a rail connection to the outside world until 1882 when the CNJ built north to Nolan's Point on the lake. Ironically, this was also the peak year of ore traffic on the line because the mines with higher quality ore, in the Mesabi Mountain Range near the Great Lakes, were just opening. So the mines in this area of New Jersey were abandoned around 1890.

This branch had a savior, however, none other than the world famous Thomas A. Edison, who tried to make a go out of it in the iron ore refining business. He went to Ogden, the town at the end of the line, and proceeded to build a huge complex that would utilize the finest modern technology to refine the low grade ore to a higher quality right at the mine head. This, he thought, would save the local mines from the advantage the midwestern mines had, which was mainly in their water borne transit to the furnaces in Indiana, Ohio, and Pennsylvania. Since the Mesabi mine ore still had to be refined at the furnace before usage, this was where Edison thought he might have a chance to increase the competitive potential of the local mines.

The people of Odgen were so taken with this plan that they renamed their town Edison. Edison himself gave up on the venture in 1900 after losing over three million dollars on the project, and the town became a ghost town. With no other traffic on the upper reaches of the line except for some logging operations and seasonal ice trains, it was eventually abandoned in 1935.

Today, the park has picnic tables, shelters, rest rooms, public phones, water and bicycle racks. There is parking for cars and horse trailers, plus RV and tent camping sites. There is also a ballfield and horseshoe pits. There are approximately eight miles of trails on the reservation which form many loops. The non-railroad trails can be steep and rocky, with an elevation change of nearly 400 feet (from 1,000 to 1,388 feet above sea-level).

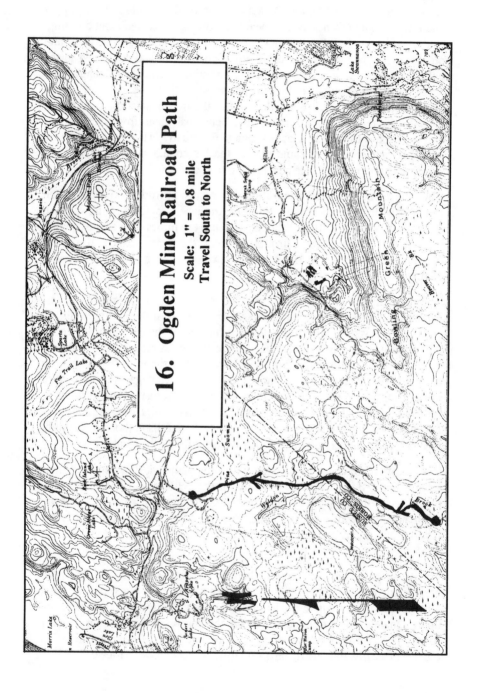

16. Ogden Mine Railroad Path

Scale: 1" = 0.8 mile
Travel South to North

Heading South from the Parking Lot

0.0 miles: Coming out of the parking lot, pass the yellow gate at the south end near the sign board. This dirt road is the rail-trail. Some original ballast can be seen here.

0.2 miles: Saffins Pond is now visible on the left as you are on a fill about 20 feet tall providing some height above the wetlands on the right. Basically down grade.

0.3 miles: Into a bit of a rock-cut as the trail bends to the right. Look for the dam at the south end of Saffins Pond. This is accessible by way of the easy path.

0.5miles: On a big fill about 35 feet tall. Note the bulldozed ties off to the side as you head down grade.

0.7 miles: The trail ends at Weldon Road. Just before this, the trail passes between the concrete walls of what uses to be a gate. The dirt road continues down and to the left from which various other trails can be used to form loops back to the parking lot. The abandoned railroad grade continues straight onto a cinder fill up to the guard rail.

Tranquil scenery at the south end of the Ogden Mine Railroad Path

117

Mountain bikers heading for the non-railroad park trails

Heading North from the Parking Lot

0.1 miles: Going past a bit of a swamp and wetlands on the right, but you are still in a hardwood forest. Look for the stone retaining wall built to hold the railroad right-of-way intact above the wetlands.

0.2 miles: Trail straightens out into a pleasant, open path.

0.4 miles: Look at this interesting rock formation that was pushed out of the way by the railroad.

0.7 miles: Wetlands on each side makes the trail into a causeway.

0.8 miles: Into a small cut that can be muddy at times.

1.2 miles: Heading north, the trail continues along a pond, and through some minor cuts.

1.4 miles: On a bit of a fill, the trail passes a dual height culvert system. Both are about 18 inches in diameter. One is on top of another to provide an added measure of drainage.

1.7 miles: The trail ends at Hayward Road and there is no parking access at this point.

17 Patriots' Path

Rockaway Valley Railroad

Endpoints: Speedwell Park to Sunrise Lake in Morristown
Location: Morris County, Morristown
Length: 5.1 miles
Surface: Asphalt, cinder and gravel
Map(s): Morristown and Mendham in the U.S.G.S. 1:24,000 series, and
Newark in the 1:100,000 series.
Uses: All non-motorized uses.

To get there: Start at Speedwell Park which is located north of downtown
Morristown on Route 202. Trail-head is on the west side of the highway
with ample parking.

Contact:
Morris County Park Commission
P.O. Box 1295 Morristown, NJ 07962-1295. 973-326-7600

Local Lodging:
Westin-Morristown Hotel, 2 Whipanny Rd., Morristown, NJ 07960.
973-539-7300
Madison Hotel, 1 Convent Rd., Morristown, NJ 07960. 973-285-1800

Local resources for bike repair/rentals:
Marty's Reliable Cycle, 173 Speedwell Avenue, Morristown, NJ 07960.
973-538-7773

The Rockaway Valley Railroad Company was incorporated in 1888 to build
a 25-mile line from the Central New Jersey Railroad (CNJ) mainline at
White House, New Jersey, and heading north through New Germantown,
Potterville, Peapack, and Mendham, up to the swampy area at Watnong and
on to the outskirts of Morristown. With the likelihood of extremely high
construction costs associated with getting past the ledges at Speedwell Lake,
the line ended at Watnong.

Here, stage-coaches transported waiting passengers and general cargo into
downtown Morristown. This free service was immediately appreciated by
the merchants of Morristown who were used to having to pay for such
service from the competing Lackawanna Railroad's nearest freight-house.

Morristown merchants and the railroad entered into a special marketing and promotional partnership in 1897. They arranged for shopping trips via rail to the business district where very special sales were advertised. Passengers were transported free of charge on the appointed day and a stage coach service brought the shoppers from the Speedwell Avenue Station to the downtown area. It was said that more than 500 folks from the small communities up the line took advantage of the offer.

As we've seen in the history of other New Jersey railroads which became rail-trails, whenever the major commodity disappeared, the railroad was abandoned. On the majority of other railroads that commodity was either milk, coal, or an ore such as zinc or iron. Here on the "Rock-a-Bye Baby" Railroad, however, that major source of revenue was bushels of peaches. At the peak of the harvests in the late 1890s, over 400,000 bushels were loaded onto trains, and that was just from the New Germantown and White House areas. A one-day record high of 72 cars full of peaches was set in 1896.

In 1904, the Rockaway Valley Railroad (RVRR) and the Speedwell Lake Railroad joined together in a corporate way which set the stage for the final few years of operation. Of course, the Speedwell Lake RR was only a "paper railroad" (one that existed only on paper in an office somewhere) and the plans to complete the extension to the Lake area were moving along. In 1910, the Morris County Traction Line (an inter-city trolley) was extended out of the downtown area to Speedwell Avenue. The RVRR saw this as an opportunity and pressed ahead to provide a connection for its passengers. Of course, it was also seen as a way to discontinue the free shuttle service with the stage coaches.

So, the Rockaway Valley RR started the big dig that was to get through the hilly and ledge-strewn area at Speedwell. Unfortunately, the work was stopped in 1912 when the construction contractor stopped receiving timely payments and pulled his crews off the job. Declining traffic levels elsewhere on the railroad hurt the cash-flow. The all-important connection with the outside world at White House Station grew tenuous when the CNJ demanded cash-on-delivery for freight cars being interchanged there.

Matters deteriorated in early 1913, when a fire destroyed much of the RVRR infrastructure in Watnong and operations ceased in October of that year. The line was eventually sold at auction to Frank B. Allen who then arranged for government funding to help him rebuild the line with heavier duty track and ties. He kept promising that operations would resume "any day now," but of course they never did. And so, in July of 1917, Allen supervised the dismantling of the line. The crew used Allen's Model-T Ford outfitted with railroad wheels to pull a small trailer on which the rails were neatly stacked and sold at a premium to the wartime scrap dealers.

"HIGH IRON"

"High Iron" is one of America's not-so-secret weapons. It is a railroadman's term for the 230,000 miles of mainline track — built, paid for and kept up by the railroads — which knit America together. • Over these strong highways of steel moves America's might — three quarters of all intercity transportation, 90% of all war freight. • In this mass movement of freight — a movement that far exceeds anything moved before by any means of transport — lies a vital lesson. • The lesson is this: America needs and must have — for success in war, for prosperity in peace — the low-priced, mass transportation which only railroads can deliver.

ASSOCIATION OF
AMERICAN RAILROADS
All United for Victory

One other interesting footnote to history is that the Historic Speedwell Park is the site of the old Speedwell Iron Works which later became the Vail Factory, which built the first telegraph. Invented by Samuel Morse in 1838, but perfected by Alfred Vail, the first message sent was, *"A patient waiter is no loser."* The ruins of this factory can be seen at the start of the trail near the dam which spans Speedwell Lake. Speedwell Village, a re-creation of an early 1800s town, is just up the road to the north and is worth a visit. Call (973) 540-0211. The following is from a brochure about the Morris County Trail System, which operates one of the best systems of trails in any eastern state.

The Patriots' Path is a gradually developing network of hiking, biking, and equestrian trails, linking many parks, watershed lands, and historic sites across southern Morris County. Much of the Path lies along the corridors of the Whippany and Black Rivers and the South Branch of the Raritan. The lower Whippany has suffered for years from industrial and sewage pollution but is slowly being brought back to life. The Black and South branches of the Raritan, on the other hand, are two of the most pristine trout streams in the state.

The surface of the Patriots' Path treadway varies with locality and terrain. Two miles of paved path run from Lake Road to Washington Valley Road in Morris Township. Other sections are stabilized with crushed stone and gravel, and still others are left as narrow paths on earth and rock.

17. Patriots' Path

Scale: 1" = 1.6 miles
Travel East to West

0.0 miles: Starting out, the trail surface is an old paving job. The asphalt is bumpy and demands your attention as you go along the left-hand side of the lake.

0.2 miles: The asphalt disappears and a dirt treadway emerges. There are also signs of old small-sized ballast. This probably dates back to the original railroad. A canopy of sycamore trees provides shade here.

0.4 miles: Grade crossing of Lake Valley Drive. This is accomplished by going up a short hill, onto the road, bearing to the left and over the bridge which spans the Whippany River, and then riding down again to the trail. Looking behind you towards the Whippany, it is hard to imagine the old wooden bent timber trestle that used to cross the river. It was pulled out by the Civilian Conservation Corps (CCC) in 1934 to enhance the scenic beauty of the tranquil setting.

0.6 miles: You are now going past the Morristown Recycling Center. The Watnong rail yard stood in this area. In January of 1913, some vandals broke into a car of flour and set fire to everything around. The freight station, two cars of merchandise (one of beer), and the coal yard and its transloading facility were all burned that night.

1.7 miles: Grade crossing of Inamere Road. The Whippany River is still our companion, meandering through the forest. A parking area is located here.

2.1 miles: There is a somewhat interesting triple culvert here. Built with 6 x 6 timbers, it is a triple type that is not seen anywhere else. The Whippany River is free flowing in this area.

2.2 miles: Grade crossing of Sussex Avenue. This is a busy road, so take care in riding. You are now back to a gravel/cinder type base. A quite elevated right-of-way through the marsh here; some ancient ties can be seen along here.

3.0 miles: Grade crossing Washington Valley Road.

3.5 miles: Grade crossing Whitehead Road. Offers a small parking area for trail users here. The trail tends to open up with some beautiful vistas of farms and meadows.

3.7-4.0 miles: Up a steep grade into the woods and winding back and forth to the top.

4.6 miles: Going downhill through the forest. Watch for horses on this section.

4.7 miles: You're now on a steep embankment that provides an interesting view of the Whippany River about 70 feet below.

5.1 miles: Trail takes a sharp bend and crosses a pressure-treated bridge that is obviously designed to allow for the safe passage of horses. The trail-head is upon you now at Sunrise Lake at Mendham Road.

EQUIPPED WITH AUTOMATIC ELECTRIC BLOCK SIGNALS.

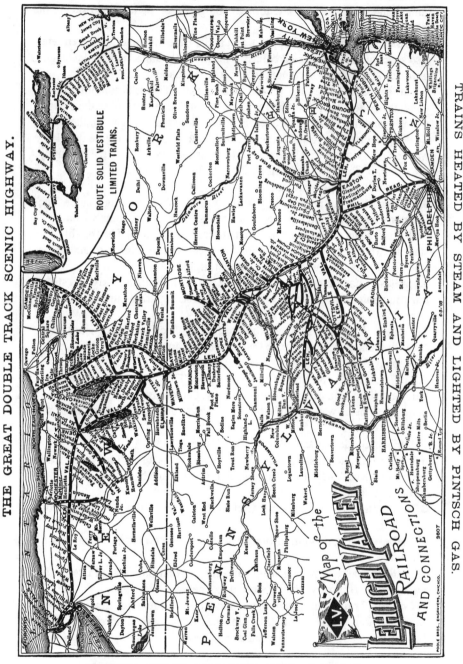

18 Paulinskill Valley Trail
New York, Susquehanna & Western Railroad (NYS&W)

Endpoints: Columbia to Sparta Junction
Location: Sussex and Warren Counties
Length: 27.3 miles
Surface: Cinder and gravel
Map(s): Portland, Blairstown, Flatbrookville, Newton West, and Newton East in the U.S.G.S. 1:24,000 series. Allentown and Middletown in the 1:100,000 series.
Uses: All non-motorized uses.

To get there: Start at the western end near the town of Columbia on the Delaware River. From I-80, take Route 94 north one mile and then right onto Brugler Road. After going over a small narrow bridge, you will find the trail-head on the left. To park, continue to the next intersection, turn right on Warrington Road, cross the Paulinskill River and park on the left in a small lot.

Contact:
Kittatinny Valley State Park
P.O. Box 621, Andover, NJ 07821. 973-786-6445

Local Bed & Breakfast:
Millers Cottage, Millbrook Road, Hope, NJ 07844. 908-459-5622
The Inn at Millrace Pond, 313 Johnsonburg Rd, Hope, NJ 07844. 908-459-4884

Local resources for bike repair/rentals:

Andover Cycle Center, Route 206, Andover, NJ 07821. 973-786-6350.
Coyote Bike'N Ski, 9 Main St., Sparta, NJ 07871. 973-729-8993

The first rail line in this area was built by John I. Blair. In 1876, he started construction of a steam railroad going west out of Blairstown to the river at Columbia and named it, not surprisingly, "The Blairstown Railroad." In 1881, the Midland Railroad (a forerunner to the New York Susquehanna & Western Railroad, NYS&W) bought the line to extend its own line from Jersey City. When a bridge was built over the Delaware River in 1882, this line was a natural to bring desirable anthracite coal from Pennsylvania to the markets in New York and New England.

The Lehigh & New England Railroad (L&NE) saw fit to obtain trackage rights from the NYS&W and run on the line from Hainesburg Junction all the way out to Swartswood Junction, a distance of about 19 miles. (*Trackage Rights* is an agreement between two railroads that allows one to travel on the tracks of another. Payment for this privilege is usually money, though sometimes an arrangement is made to reciprocate in a similar fashion at another location.) After the L&NE pulled out in 1961, there wasn't enough NYS&W traffic to sustain the line, and it was abandoned totally shortly thereafter.

In 1962, the rails and ties were pulled up and the ROW languished as an unofficial trail for decades. (See page 20 for a history of the hard work that was required to develop this trail.) Today, after the efforts of the Paulinskill Valley Trail Committee, the trail is the anchor of the network of open and under-development projects in New Jersey.

The following is reprinted from the introduction of the book, *Paulinskill Valley: Before & After*, written by Len Frank, President, Paulinskill Valley Trail Committee.

Abandoned by the New York Susquehanna and Western Railroad in 1962, the trail was purchased by the City of Newark for a possible future water conduit to connect the proposed Tocks Island Dam reservoir with the Pequannock Watershed. The cinder base trail traverses two counties for 27 miles, has an average width of 66 feet and a total area of 102 acres.

Numerous historic artifacts can still be seen along the trail, including six remnants of the original nine creameries and ice houses that serviced the railroad, numerous station foundations, eight railroad bridges, cattle passes, battery boxes, whistle markers, and mileage markers. Fishing access is provided by six river bridges where roads cross the trail. The trail parallels the river for much of its length and provides canoeists with access to the Paulinskill River.

The trail interconnects with:
· The Columbia Lakes Management Area in Knowlton
· The Delaware Water Gap National Recreation Area and the Appalachian Trail
· The Lackawanna Cut Off and the Lehigh & New England right-of-way
· The Sussex Branch Trail, which is managed by the Kittatinny Valley State Park

In a number of areas, the trail provides a buffer zone between Paulinskill River and threatened development. The trail is an integral part of the Paulinskill Watershed and is important for the protection of the river. Since 1962, the trail has been used by outdoor enthusiasts as a multipurpose trail. Users include hikers, bikers, horse-back riders, cross-country skiers, joggers, fishermen, hunters, and canoeists. Since the trail is mostly level, the right-of-way also provides opportunities for use by the very young, the disabled, and the elderly. Wildlife, such as otter, beaver, muskrat, mink, and deer, can be seen from the trail, as well as many species of birds which visit the area or nest along the way. In addition to a wide variety of trees and shrubs, many wild flowers and ferns grow along the side of the trail including several rare and endangered species. Thirty-five recreational and environmental organizations have supported the public acquisition of the property for use as an all-weather, year-round trail. Through the efforts of the Paulinskill Valley Trail Committee the trail was purchased by New Jersey Green Acres and became a state park on Oct. 3, 1992.

The Paulinskill Viaduct

How Many Trains Ran Through the Paulinskill Valley?
By Harold S. Fredericks

It depended on the year, the season, and the day. Let's pick 1916 for the year. There were more railroad miles in the U.S. during that year than any other. Let's pick the summer; there was more general activity, and for sure there was an ice train. Then we pick a day in midweek, so we have July 12, 1916. In that year, according to Moody's Manual of Railroads, the Susquehanna Railroad owned 98 locomotives, 105 passenger cars, 501 freight and box cars, 1710 coal cars, one flat car, and 72 service cars, including cabooses.

The 1916 New York Susquehanna & Western timetable showed 2 passenger trains going through the valley to Stroudsburg. We have no timetable of coal trains, so let's make a calculated estimate. The railroad hauled nearly one and a half million tons of anthracite per year. This tonnage would require four 25-car coal trains per day.

We know that there was a way freight that stopped at all of the freight houses and switched cars in and out of the local sidings. There was also at least one through freight that exchanged cars at Hainesburg Junction and Sparta Junction. There was an ice train that came from the Poconos and supplied creameries along the line and filled ice houses as far as Jersey City. The milk train picked up milk at the many milk platforms between Stroudsburg and Beaver Lake. It is safe to add one or more which might be a single engine going to or coming from the shops for repair, or a work train, or even an inspection train. Let's not forget the Dinky that made two trips daily between Blairstown and Delaware. [The dinky was a self-propelled 'rail-bus' of the era. On some railroads this would be called a Doodlebug.] This adds up to 13 Susquehanna trains.

In 1916, the Lehigh & New England (LNE) Railroad shipped much more coal than did the Susquehanna; some of the coal was diverted to the Philadelphia area. The LNE had heavier engines and longer trains. Without accurate figures, we make a guesstimate of five LNE coal trains daily going to New England. LNE passenger trains came to Swartswood, but did not traverse the Paulinskill Valley. Probably two freight trains did go through. So we add seven LNE trains to the 13 Susquehanna trains, making 20 trains. Remember, though, all of these trains have to return, giving us a total of 40 trains passing through the Paulinskill Valley daily.

How did the dispatcher schedule 40 trains on a single track railroad with no more mishaps than actually occurred? There were plans to double track the railroad in 1916, but this never did happen. Many through trains went at night, first in one direction and then the other. Of course, there were meets where one train would take the siding while the other train would pass. The two longest sidings on the railroad were in Blairstown (which held 63 cars) and Stillwater (which held 65 cars).

Let's turn back time to July 12, 1916, and stand along the track at Vail Station and watch the trains. We see Atlantic type steam engines hauling varnished passenger, mail, and express cars; and mogul type engines with a string of colorful box cars and the classic caboose. We see twenty-five loaded coal cars behind double headed consolidated type locomotives. The trains are gone, but we can visualize them as we walk the path that they rode on.

The story you have just read was reprinted from The Paulinskill Signal, a newsletter of the Paulinskill Valley Trail Committee, P.O. Box 7076, Hackettstown, NJ 07840.

Trail marker on the Paulinskill Valley Trail (photo by Susan Data-Samtak)

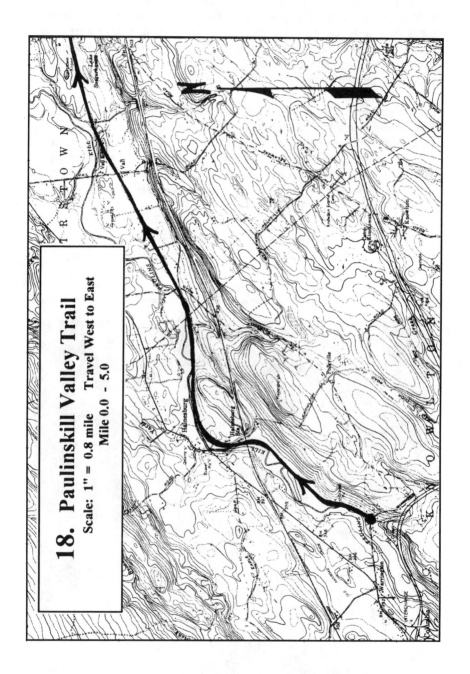

18. **Paulinskill Valley Trail**

Scale: 1" = 0.8 mile   Travel West to East

Mile 0.0 - 5.0

130

0.0 miles: A sign at the start says *The Paulinskil Valley Trail: line was in service for various ownerships from 1876 to 1961.* Here at the start, it is grass covered and the trail is actually shared with a farmer who uses it to access his nearby fields.

0.8 miles: A small sign installed by Harold Frederick (the first of many you'll encounter) points out that Hainesburg Junction once stood here. The decaying remains of some old structures are all that is seen, though one can imagine the bustling activity that took place. A two-story combination freight and passenger station was also among the structures on this site. This station was closed as an agency in 1938 and was sold to a local business in 1951. (An "agency" was an official railroad term denoting a location where passenger tickets could be purchased and/or freight could be shipped. Such a place was usually staffed full-time.) One of many rail-served creameries was also in this immediate area. Another small white sign announces that the Lehigh and New England Railroad, (LNE) 1890-1962, and the New York, Susquehanna & Western, (NYS&W or Susie Q) 1876-1961 joined here at Hainesburg.

1.1 miles: The Paulinskill River is adjacent, as is the Paulinskill Viaduct. This was one the "wonders of the world" when built by the Lackawanna Railroad in 1909. Over 1,100 feet long and towering 115 feet above the valley floor, its concrete arches were a symbol of the Lackawanna's grand vision. A similarly impressive one crosses the Delaware River about 3 miles west. The Paulinskill Viaduct was the largest such structure in the world until Lackawanna built a larger one in Pennsylvania. (see the next ride, #19, for more information on this). Also visible here is the turntable pit -- owned by the LNE -- which allowed the locomotives to be turned for their trip back home. It is interesting to note that, though the NYS&W owned the track, the largest number of trains to pass this way were LNE-owned using a trackage rights agreement (tenant-landlord), with the Susie Q. Just after the viaduct, Station Road runs parallel to the trail for about half a mile.

1.6 miles: Road and rail-trail divide now.

1.7 miles: Still parallel to the Paulinskill are some old telegraph poles which are intact, but missing their insulators.

2.3 miles: Agricultural grade crossing is here and the power lines diverge from the trail. Look to the west for a good view of Kittatinny Mountain.

2.4 miles: Crossing a small tributary of the Paulinskill via a pressure-treated deck bridge that is newly constructed. The abutments are of railroad heritage. This is known on some trail maps as bridge # 9. Just after the bridge, you'll come out onto Polkville Road.

3.2 miles: Grade crossings of a private driveway through a farm. Next, for about two-tenths of a mile, you'll be on a dirt road which eventually curves away.

Bridge over the Paulinskill River at Marksboro

3.7 miles: Walnut Valley Road grade crossing. There are some old buildings here, a former creamery and a feed store. Both were rail-served at one time. This was the area known on railroad timetables as Vails. A small station stood here at one time, though it was not the original one the railroad had in mind. Wait till you get to Kalarama in about 2 miles for more information.

4.0 miles: Trail is on a small fill that is more of a shelf, with hillside up to the left and down to the right.

4.1 miles: Still on the shelf fill, but it opens up to a normal fill about 25 feet high. A culvert is underneath also.

4.2 miles: Grade crossing of Gwinnup Road. The house adjacent to the trail has a couple of whistle markers on the site. The driveway is the RoW of the railroad, so please stay just to the north of the driveway and do not intrude on the trail's neighbor. Mile-marker sign here is marked *0.4 miles to Vail* and *1.1 miles to Kalarama Airport.* Today the Airport is known as the Blairstown Airport.

5.2 miles: You are now at the approach to the airport and on a fill with corn fields on the left.

5.4 miles: Trail runs adjacent to the airport. From the mid-1940s to 1955, the old NYS&W ran an annual employee picnic excursion train out here. Leaving Jersey City early in the morning and stopping at all the major crew areas along the way, it would pick up employees and their families for a day's fun in the sun at the large grassy meadows of the Blairstown Airport and nearby Lake Susquehanna. Hot dogs, soda, sports, and a large tent were the order of the day. All the stops were pulled out, and every year it was a memorable trip for all.

5.7 miles: You are now at the far end of the airport, going on a small access road. This was the site of the Kalarama Station. In 1891, the NYS&W wanted to move it to Vails, so they jacked it up onto timbers and put it on the rails. They slowly pulled it with a locomotive towards Vails until disaster struck. It slid off the rails and tumbled down an embankment where it became a source of fuel for wood-stoves in the area and a source of embarrassment for the Susie Q.

5.9 miles: Into a small cut here and then out onto the shelf again with the hill up to the right.

6.6 miles: Agricultural grade crossing with some pleasant farm vistas on the left and woods on the right.

6.8 miles: A large meadow on the left with a hillside on the right. A fairly wide RoW indicates that there may have been double track in this area.

7.0 miles: Down below to the left you'll see a large horse training area.

7.1 miles: Agricultural grade crossing here leads to the paddock. More lovely meadows.

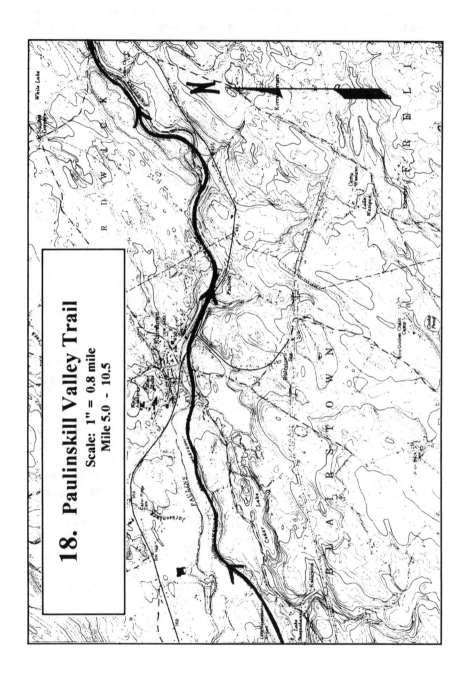

18. Paulinskill Valley Trail

Scale: 1" = 0.8 mile

Mile 5.0 - 10.5

134

7.2 miles: The river is seen again down on the left as you go across another agricultural grade crossing.

7.3 miles: You are now passing through Foot-Bridge Park in Blairstown. This is a large, open air park with the usual amenities. Blairstown was the terminus for the Blairstown Railroad, constructed by John I. Blair. The parking area used to be a yard area for the railroad, and it had a large two-story passenger station as well as an "Armstrong" turntable. (A turntable was like a giant lazy-Susan, turning steam locomotives to face the correct direction of travel. An "Armstrong" turntable denotes a manually operated, non-electric turntable. These were usually operated by men with strong arms.) This area also had a dense network of railroad-associated buildings and industries, such as a lumber yard, coal dealer, creamery, and L.C.L. Freight house. (Less than Car Load, meaning less than *full* car load. This would be the place where you went to pickup your items that were delivered through the Railway Express Agency, a forerunner of UPS.) It's hard to imagine such a conglomeration of buildings today as you stand in the middle of the parking lot. Everything was torn down when the town was preparing for the nation's bicentennial in 1976. The plan at the time was to knock down all the old structures to make room for a park celebrating the history of the nation.

7.6 miles: Crossing under Route 94. Here the RoW is in good condition as you travel on a fill for a moment and then into the woods again.

8.0 miles: Look on the adjacent Paulinskill and you'll see a scenic dam. On the steep hillside on the left are some cast-off ties.

8.3 miles: Paulina, a small flag-stop station in years gone by, is located here. Today it is the home of Paulina Park, which has a dam on the Paulinskill. Parking for trail users is located here. An interesting highway bridge with a wooden deck is nearby also. Right after the bridge, into a small shalestone cut.

8.7 miles: Wetlands exist on both sides with extensive wildflowers and an occasional frog is heard. Thru-plate girder bridge # 7 is here also, crossing over the Paulinskill. Shortly some rapids will appear in the river.

8.8 miles: Mile-marker here says JC81-- Jersey City 81 miles farther. This is one of the unusual triangular constructed markers only seen in NJ. This type of construction may have been used to provide a measure of strength and longevity (3-sides are stronger than 2).

9.0 miles: Just before entering a cut, a burbling brook goes under the trail by way of a culvert.

9.3 miles: Another crossing of the Paulinskill. Same construction as before: nice pressure-treated decking with side rails about 3-4 feet high. Consider this one to be bridge # 6.

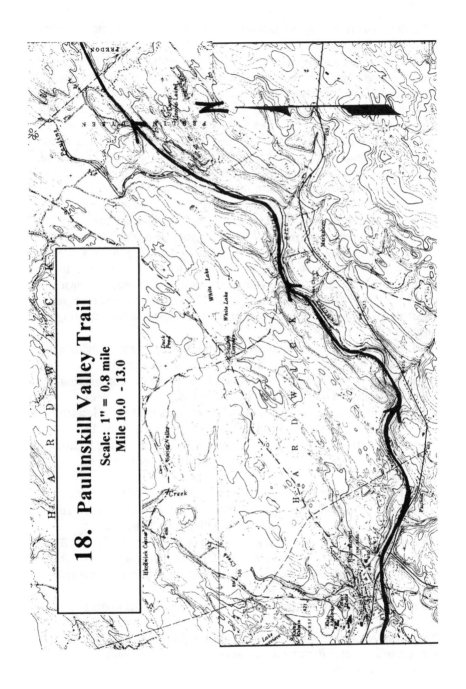

18. Paulinskill Valley Trail
Scale: 1" = 0.8 mile
Mile 10.0 - 13.0

9.8 miles: Crossing through another shelf with the uphill side being cut away to expose an interesting rock face about 15 feet high which also has some trees growing out of it. The river is on the right. Large amounts of ballast used as a filled-in repair job are evidence of a major washout that dates back to Hurricane Diane in 1955. An interesting telegraph pole with provisions for ten insulator mountings; none of which are intact, however.

10.0 miles: A small cut here as the river transforms into a series of pools and rapids.

10.5 miles: Parking is available here at Spring Valley Road. This is on the old railroad maps as Marksboro, site of a small flag-stop station and another of Mr. Frederick's signs. This one marks the site as *Marksboro*.

10.6 miles: Concrete wall on the left is evidence of a creamery and ice house in days gone by. A spur from here led to White Lake, just over the hill where the ice was harvested.

11.0 miles: Agricultural grade crossing which leads to a large meadow on the left.

11.2 miles: Crossing the river once again, this time by way of an attractive through-truss bridge. This one is unusual in that it has curved bracing. For many years, this was a major road-block because of a missing deck. In 1997, the deck was completed and now we don't have to detour onto roads.

12.3 miles: Grade crossing at Stillwater Road.

12.7 miles: Grade crossing at Henfoot Road. A gentleman farmer's backyard is traversed by the trail which in this area is part grass and part cinder/coal. Beautifully manicured grounds surround you, so don't deviate from the path and make the family uncomfortable. Shortly you'll be back into the woods. It is likely you'll encounter horses on this next section, so be aware.

13.0 miles: On a bit of a fill which is about 20 feet tall and constructed of cinder; then a shelf appears which is higher on the right and low to the left.

13.5 Genuine semaphore signal tower here is without its blades and is very rusted but nonetheless an eerie sight. *Erected in 1909* says the sign erected by Harold Frederick. Look to the left to see the remains of a lime kiln.

13.7 miles: Wetlands and ponds on the left have Great Blue Herons, so be on the lookout for them.

14.0 miles: Grade crossing of Cedar Ridge Road. This is adjacent to the Water Wheel Farm, which is an equestrian boarding farm (phone number (973) 383-3409). This is the site of the "Golden Spike" ceremony which took place on October 3, 1992. Hikers from Columbia and hikers from Sparta met here, and the spike was driven into an old Susquehanna wooden tie, thus commemorating the official purchase of the corridor by the state.

14.5 miles: Whistle marker is seen here, as are some derelict telegraph poles. Look carefully off into the woods and you'll see some bird houses put there by a neighbor.

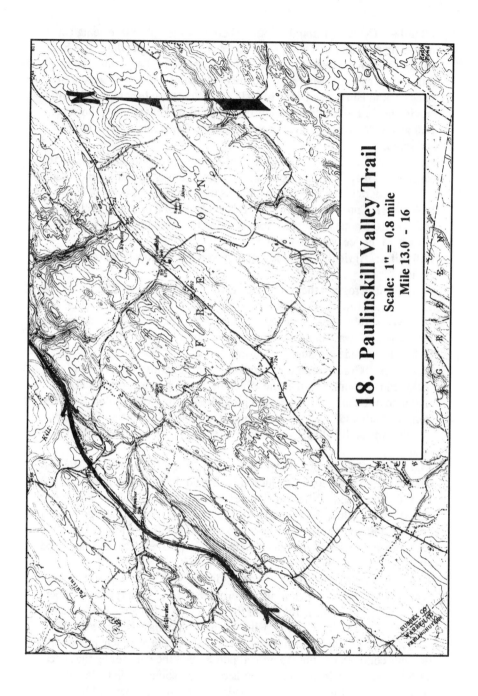

18. Paulinskill Valley Trail
Scale: 1" = 0.8 mile
Mile 13.0 - 16

138

14.6 miles: Grade crossing at Wall Street.

14.9 miles: Cut here is low to the left with rocky ledge rising steeply to the right. Trail will swing to the right here also.

15.0 miles: Grade crossing of Old Station Road. This is the site of the old Stillwater Station, operated by the NYS&W until 1962, when the railroad was pulled out. It burned to the ground shortly after.

15.5 miles: On a bit of a fill here with a stream to the right and meadows to the left.

15.6 miles: Shallow cut with round stones. Be prepared to make a slight jog in the trail here where a grade crossing intersects. A bridge used to be here but has been filled in so you have to go up a hill, cross County Route 610, and then down onto the trail again. Just on the other side of the road is a derelict old building that used to be the home of the Fulbaum Dairy Company, a regular shipper of milk on the railroad. Stillwater used to have another dairy, McDermatt Dairy. Every community on the line had at least one and sometimes more. Borden had three thriving creameries on the line.

15.8 miles: Many cedar trees here as well as a small fill about 8 feet high.

16.1 miles: Fairly big shelf here with a steep embankment down to the river on the left and a hill up to the right.

16.4 miles: Grade crossing of Kohlbocker Road.

16.7 miles: Sign says "bridge out." A quick down and then up to get past where the bridge used to span West End Road Route 614. A nice park here, as well as a dam and beach. This is the former site of Emmons Station.

17.4 miles: Overlooking a beautiful lake that has high use by recreational boaters. You are on a shelf with the heights to the right, and you are still high above the water.

17.8 miles: A big fill about 25-30 feet high located here above some waterfront properties.

18.0 miles: Passing through a 30-foot high cut.

18.1 miles: A 30-foot high fill located here allows you to survey the surroundings. The material for this fill was probably gathered from the cut ahead at 22.9 miles.

18.9 miles: An old foundation here is all that remains of a creamery that had a bottling plant here as well.

19.1 miles: Concrete flooring is all that remains of Swartswood Station. Fairly small at 24 x 16 feet, it was taken down in 1962. Visible just ahead on the right are the remains of the water tank. Built into the hillside with cement construction of the lower section, it is very unique. No wooden components remain. The water tank was situated to provide replenishment for northbound trains heading over the mountain. The passenger cars behind would then line up right at the platform for the passenger station. Just ahead are the footings for the phantom bridge over the adjacent County Route 622. These are all that remains of the crossing over the road.

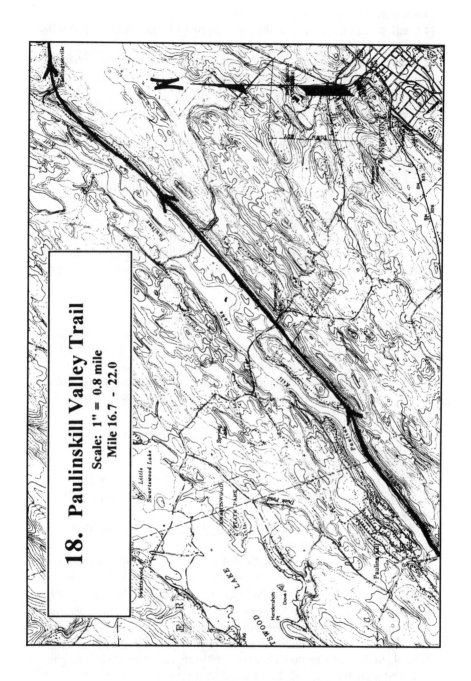

18. Paulinskill Valley Trail

Scale: 1" = 0.8 mile
Mile 16.7 - 22.0

19.3 miles: Here lie the derelict remains of the Swartswood Junction telegraph office. Also in this area are the remains of a 61-foot turntable pit. This was used to turn the Lehigh & New England (LNE) engine on the passenger train that ran from Goshen New York to Swartswood. This ran as a full train until the late 1920s when it was downsized to a self-propelled rail-bus type train called a Gas Brill Car. Passenger service ended during the depression in 1937.

19.5 miles: The diverging path at this point is actually the LNE pulling away to the northeast as we take a more eastward course on the alignment of the NYS&W. The LNE RoW here is not open as a trail at this time.

20.1 miles: A small rock-cut is here, higher on the right and lower on the left. Then a small culvert with a big waterfall in the background as you are on a 40-foot high fill. Grade crossing ahead is over Plotts Road.

21.1 miles: Drainage structure on the right on the hill above is a set of stones placed to divert water from the RoW.

21.5 miles: Power lines crossing the trail bring you into the sun and then into the woods again.

21.7 miles: Massive shale cut about 40 feet high and then onto a fill about the same height.

21.9 miles: Abandoned farm and outbuilding with road just beyond trees.

22.1 miles: Site of the old Halsey Station. Old Stage Coach Road and Halsey Road are nearby. Grade crossing of Route 519.

22.6 miles: Uncle Chuck's Pizza is here for your dining pleasure.

22.7 miles: PVRT sign says Warbasse is 1.8 miles ahead.

23.8 miles: Intersection of Route 94 and Taylor Road Crossing here used to be by bridge over the highway. Today it is a steep down and then up for the trail users.

24.5 miles: On a big long fill, the start of the downward grade to Warbasse.

24.7 miles: Some more abandoned agricultural buildings which are part of the old Hyper-Humus complex. In 1915, a company by the name of Hyper-Humus was formed to market and bag the huge peat deposits found along this area. This was one of the country's largest deposits of the "black gold," which is used in gardens and farms. Hyper-Humus is still in business today.

25.0 miles : Crossing the Paulinskill once more on a 60-foot plate girder bridge which has a new pressure-treated deck, and then on to Warbasse Junction where the Sussex Branch Trail (see Ride # 21) intersects with the Paulinskill Trail. Just beyond are the remains of a smash board.

A smash board was a rudimentary railroad stop sign resembling a gate across the right-of-way. The NYS&W train crew was obliged to stop, get out, unlock the gate, and the remote dispatcher would display to the Lackawanna Railroad a STOP signal on the semaphore boards. The NYS&W train would then proceed to the hazard area, look for approaching trains, lock the gate behind them, and then proceed through.

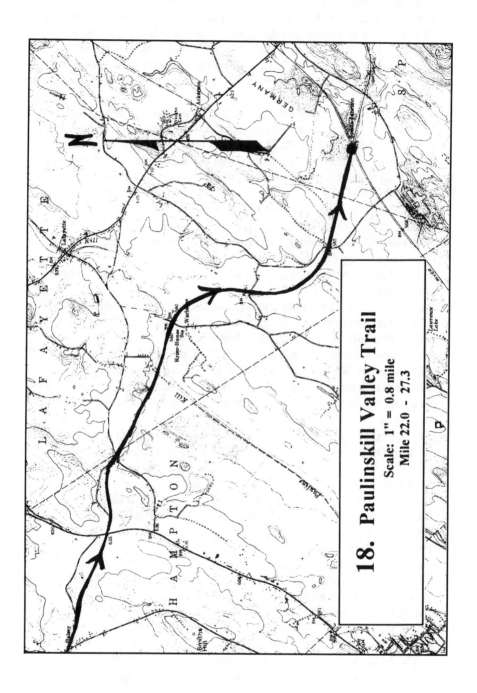

18. Paulinskill Valley Trail

Scale: 1" = 0.8 mile

Mile 22.0 - 27.3

25.1 miles: Genuine NYS&W concrete mile marker inscribed with JC-65. It was in this area that a passing siding was constructed to allow trains to pass one another. The passenger station was just north of the diamond.

25.2 miles: Here is the junction where the Franklin Branch of the Lackawanna crossed at grade. A marker notes that the Franklin Branch was in operation from 1869 to 1934. The primary reason for going to Franklin was the iron furnaces and related mining industry there.

25.7 miles: Crossing a small stream known as Morris Farm Lafayette via pressure treated timbers. Cut stone abutments placed in and backed up with some rip-rap. The right-of-way for the Franklin Branch of the Lackawanna is visible only a few yards away. The abutments for their bridge over the same stream are constructed of the material they liked best, concrete. Grade crossing of Garrison Road is right after the bridge.

25.8 miles: Mile-marker 64-JC, a twin to the previous marker.

26.0 miles: Wetlands on the left with the Morris Farm Lafayette stream still on the right.

26.5 miles: Horses must stop here at a grade crossing of a neighborhood lane known as Sunset Inn-Limecrest Road or County Route 623. Just after the road, other users will be crossing the stream once again. This crossing is interesting because of the less-than-desirable decking (two 20-inch timbers, that's all). If you look closely at the footings of the bridge, you'll notice that it was rebuilt after a flood. Timber abutments on the north side and stone on the south side. Also here is one of the familiar little markers that make this trail so interesting. It says *Warbasse 1.4 miles & Sparta Jct. 0.9 miles.*

27.0 miles: Crossing over the stream again. This one is hand-built by Harold Frederick (a very busy guy) and is a walking-only bridge. Note the large chunks of coal on the left side of the trail in the wetlands woods.

27.3 miles: Sparta Junction is here. The NYS&W Railroad mainline is active here. *Do Not Trespass on railroad property.* Railroad police are in the area and don't take kindly to people who fail to heed the warning. There are a number of bits of railroad archaeology you can see without getting into trouble. Still visible in the weeds is the diamond (a section of track that shaped like a diamond that allowed two railroads to cross at grade). The last of the familiar signs is here. This one is marked *Sparta Jct. on the Paulinskill Valley Trail---26 miles to Columbia. Limecrest Spur. NYS & W 1985.* The on-line industries visible here are on the main track; to the left is an M&M-Mars sweetener plant, and off of this track is a propane dealer. To the right and out of sight is a Limestone Plant. The "Susie Q" (NYS&W) comes out here only as needed, which is about once a week.

19 Pemberton Rail-Trail

Pennsylvania Railroad

Endpoints: Hanover St. in Pemberton to Birmingham Rd. in Birmingham.
Location: Burlington County, townships of Pemberton and Birmingham.
Length: *Phase 1* is **1.4 miles**. When *Phase 2* is complete, **3.0 miles** total.
Surface: Cinder and gravel. (*Phase 1* is due to be paved in the fall of 1998; *Phase 2* is due to be open in approximately 1999.)
Map(s): Pemberton, U.S.G.S. 1:24,000 series
Uses: All non-motorized uses, except horses.

To get there: From the North, take the New Jersey Turnpike to Route 206. Then take County Route 520 East into South Pemberton. Take left (north) onto Hanover Street. Follow this for about 0.5 miles and you'll see an old passenger station on the left. Park here where it is approved and safe.

Contact:
Scott England, Pemberton Rotary Club
P.O. Box 333, Pemberton, NJ 08068 (609) 265-2652

Local Bed & Breakfast:
Isaac Hilliard House Bed & Breakfast, 31 Hanover St.,
Pemberton NJ 08068 609-894-0756; 800-371-0756.
Local resources for bike repair/rentals:
Mount Holly Schwinn Bicycles,164 Route 38, Mount Holly, NJ 08060.
609-267-6620

The group most responsible for getting this trail built is the Pemberton Rotary Club. This sort of project is a natural for a community service club like the Rotary. The rail-to-trail project here was the vision of Jerry Jerome who saw a community need for better recreation and a reason for tourists to come and visit the surrounding area. He sold his fellow Rotarians on the need and they proceeded to fill that need. Their mission statement resounds with pride and purpose:

It is the desire of the Pemberton Rotary Club to take the leadership role in the plotting, developing and maintenance of a hiking and biking trail system. This non-motorized trail system would be located in a portion of Pemberton Township, Pemberton Borough and Fort Dix. The reality of such a trail system could serve as the nucleus of an east/west trail which is currently under review by the State of New Jersey.

The Pemberton Rail-Trail is mostly cinder-based and wide open

The Pemberton Rotary Club is undertaking this project with two goals as their driving force. First, bring to fruition a trail system that gives to the community a recreational resource that is natural to the community's own setting. The second goal is to bring together clubs, organizations, municipal governments, and individuals to collectively make this trail system a reality.

It's interesting that there are two in-town organizations at work here. The Rotary is in the lead to create the trail and an ad hoc citizens group called Save Our Station is in the lead to obtain funding to restore the passenger station. As of this writing, the project is nearing completion.

With a population of only 1,200 people, Pemberton Borough is a typical old-style town with friendly residents, interesting historical sites, and a quiet ambiance that invites you to pause and relax. The best time to visit the trail might be the fall when the Fall-Fest is in full swing. Here you'll find a big town fair atmosphere with many vendors selling antiques and other goods. There is a historical component as well, with reenactments of Revolutionary and Civil War engagements.

The first train ran from Nathong to Pemberton in 1861 and, by 1870, the railroad was the single largest employer in town. At that time, it served 40 businesses and 7 industries in the Pemberton. Like many other secondary lines that became rail-trails, this one had a number of owners in the early years. The usual rounds of mergers, acquisitions, and reorganizations that plagued these light density lines attracted the attention of the locally larger railroad. In this case, that railroad was none other than the Pennsylvania Railroad, otherwise known to locals as "the Pennsy." In 1883, the Pennsy merged the final small railroad, the Pemberton & Hightstown Railroad, into their system.

During the famous Blizzard of 1888, a wall of snow 10-to-20 feet high blocked the line at Pemberton for over a mile. The declining revenue caused by the railroad being out of service for so long forced Pennsy to cease operations in April of that year. A new entity called Union Transportation Company was then created and leased to the Pennsy in August of 1888.

In September 1917, Camp Dix was built and the UT-Pennsy line through Pemberton was given a new lease on life with the infusion of military traffic. During the depression, the passenger service ended but, in 1940, things turned around dramatically when the military presence at (newly renamed) Fort Dix was upgraded in preparation for the coming war.

During World War II, this line was used to transport thousands of troops from the training center at Fort Dix to the mainline at Camden. Here, connections were made to reach troop ships bound for the European theater of operations. In just one day in 1943, over 18,000 troops were transported through here.

After the war, things settled back into their bucolic backwater ways. In fact, it seems that the Pennsy also forgot about the UT and the Pemberton branch because, although they dieselized the rest of their huge system, steam locomotives continued to run here into the late 1950s. The Pennsylvania Railroad's last scheduled run of a steam-powered passenger train occurred on this line on November 12, 1957, when a commuter train to Camden was pulled by #5244, one of the Pennsy's famed K-4 Pacific Class locomotives. On July 14, 1959, the very last in-service steam locomotive of the Pennsylvania Railroad, a small switching engine, came out of Pemberton to go to Philadelphia for scrapping.

The dieselized UT soldiered on with declining fortunes through the merger of the Pennsylvania Railroad and the New York Central, creating Penn-Central (PC) in 1968, and through the later creation of Conrail in 1976. On March 31, 1977, the last train came through Pemberton and Conrail finally got around to abandoning the line in 1982 and pulled out the rails in 1984.

The North Pemberton Station, located at the start of the Pemberton Rail-Trail

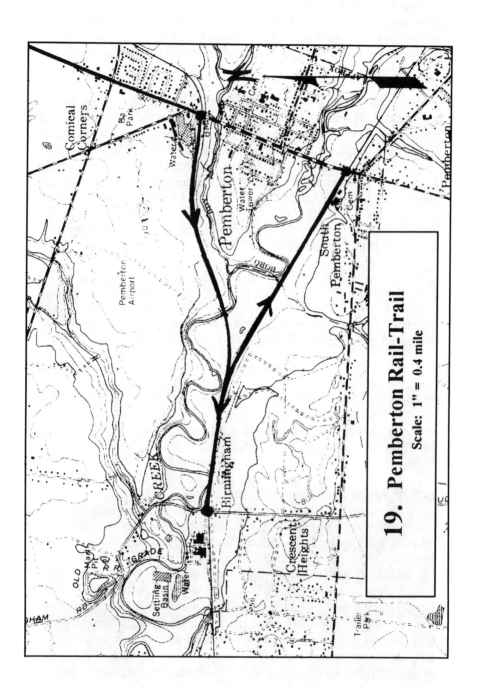

19. Pemberton Rail-Trail

Scale: 1" = 0.4 mile

0.0 miles: At the start of the trail sits the jewel of the town, the North Pemberton Station. Though a bit tarnished, the brick and stucco hip-roofed passenger station will be restored in years to come and made an essential part of Pemberton's trail. The current station was built in 1892 by the Pennsylvania Railroad and the Union Transportation Company as a replacement for the original wooden one which had burned down a year earlier. Standing on the 900-foot-long train platform and looking north, today you see an open field adjacent to the trail. In years past, this was the Pemberton yard which was about 6 tracks wide, and a company known as Presidential Homes stood across the yard. They built pre-fab homes here just before and during World War II.

0.2 miles: Going west on the trail and past a large, scenic dairy farm on the right and then large, rolling meadows

0.4 miles: Passing over a 2-foot diameter iron culvert which allows water to drain off the farm and get past the railroad's RoW.

0.5 miles: If you look closely in a clump of 30-year-old trees along the north side of the trail, you'll see a semaphore signal that is basically intact and restorable. This was called Pemberton home signal as it protected the movement of trains into the siding at the North Pemberton station as well as movements out of the yard adjacent.

0.7 miles: This is the end of the nearby farm field on the right. If you stop just before the tree line starts again and look closely at the top of the hill and meadow, you'll see a hangar which is part of the South Pemberton Airport. This place specializes in ultra-light aircraft.

0.8 miles: Sticky Ball Trees are seen in this area as well as Black Birches, Sycamores, and Black Cherry trees. Notice the large circular growths attached to the Cherry trees. This is called Black Knot Disease and it ruins the grain of the tree for veneer purposes. In Pennsylvania, which is the country's third largest producer of hardwood veneers, this is a major problem.

0.9 miles: Crossing over the North Branch of the Rancocas Creek which is about 35 feet wide. It comes in from the left and goes underneath a poured concrete bridge that dates back to 1914. Sprint has installed a conduit for their fiber optic network which shares the RoW of the trail.

1.0 miles: Here is a junction with a branch that comes off the main and swings away to the southeast. The RoW is generally open and accessible, though prone to large puddles, sand, and mud. There is also a section in private ownership, so it is not recommended that users travel on this line. This section, however, is to be upgraded as part of a *phase 2* improvement and extension to the trail system. Once that phase is completed, you will be able to travel west on the initial section, swing to the south and then east on this new section, and then head north along city streets into Pemberton Borough.

In railroad circles, this area was known as Pemberton Junction, where a small passenger station stood. During peak season, 12 trains a day carried passengers who came to vacation at the Birmingham Inn to this stop. This was one of those typical grander-than-life, ornate wooden resort hotels which were popularized around the country by quick and easy railroad connections. The station was open until 1898; then the patrons were brought in from the Birmingham Station, which was about 1.5 miles west of here. During the last years of the Depression and after a fire destroyed the local poor-house, the Inn was converted to house the local destitute folks. After World War II, the Permutit Company in Birmingham tore down the structure and today it is a ballfield.

1.1 miles: The Rancocas Creek swings in from the right and curves sharply away once again. You'll note some very large (over 30" diameter) blow-downs that span the creek, making for a natural bridge.

1.3 miles: The trail widens out, with a meadow off to the left.

1.4 miles: End of the trail within the Village of Birmingham.

In the 1800s, the village of Birmingham had a major industry based on the mineral glauconite, or greensand as it was commonly called. This mineral was strip-mined out of veins about 10 feet below the surface of the ground. Greensand, also known as marl, was first mined around 1820 and was used as a fertilizer and soil sweetener to reduce acidity. This boom ended with the introduction of synthetic fertilizers in the 1870s. Interestingly, 50 years later, in the 1920s, a resurgence occurred in the mining of the greensand when the Permutit Company came in and used the resource as a water softener. A processing plant was built in the neighborhood which used a small narrow-gauge railroad to carry the material the 0.7 miles distance from the mine to the plant. This operation ran until 1956, when the company (by then known as IONAC) finally shut it down and the mine area became a park.

At the end of the trail today, you can see in the distance the Sybron Chemical Company (descendant corporation of IONAC). They, too, make water purification equipment and a tool in the environmental clean-up field called bio-remediation. Bio-remediation came into the news during the *Exxon Valdez* clean-up off the coast of Alaska in 1989. Sybron makes a "bug" or bacteria that neutralizes or "eats" petroleum products, rendering them inert.

The local sewage treatment plant is here as well as a gate to the trail. Parking is available here and accessed by way of Birmingham Road.

20 Pequest Fish and WMA

Lehigh & Hudson River Railway (L&HR)

Endpoints : From the intersection of Routes 31 and 46 in Buttzville, to Pequest Road in Townsbury
Location: Warren County
Length: 4.1 miles
Surface: Cinder, gravel, original ballast and ties
Map(s): Washington and Belvedere in the U.S.G.S. 1:24,000 series, and Allentown and Newark in the 1:100,000 series.
Uses: All non-motorized uses. Horses by permit only.

To get there: From the intersection of State Route 31 and U.S. 46, proceed east on 46 for about 4.5 miles to Pequest Road in Townsbury. Follow Pequest Road for 0.5 miles until it crosses over the Pequest River, and park at the small lot adjacent to the bridge. The trail starts just downstream from here. Parking is also available at the Pequest Trout Hatchery access road, located on U.S. 46.

Contact:
Division of Fish, Game and Wildlife
P.O. Box 400, Trenton, NJ 08625. 609-292-2965

Local Bed & Breakfasts:
The Inn at Millrace Pond, 313 Johnsonburg Rd, Hope, NJ 07844.
908-459-4884

Local resources for bike repair/rentals:
Andover Cycle Center, Route 206, Andover, NJ 07821. 973-786-6350.
Coyote Bike'N Ski, 9 Main St., Sparta, NJ 07871. 973-729-8993

Local resources for Equestrian needs:
Upper River Valley Stables, Route 94, Lafayette 201-579-1636

Part of the following information is from a brochure published by the New Jersey RailTrails, a state-wide non-profit group that works to turn abandoned railroads into multi-use public trails. Information about joining is available by writing to P.O. Box 23, Pluckemin, NJ 07978, or by calling 215-340-9974.

Located in the Pequest Valley of Warren County, near Great Meadows, this trail is the former rail bed of the Lehigh & Hudson River Railroad. This line was a perfect example of a number of smaller railroads combining to form a larger route under one corporate entity. Constructed between 1861 and 1882, this line served as one of the "Anthracite Roads" connection into New England and was built to carry mainly coal.

The original destination was Newburg, where a car ferry across the great natural barrier served until the high bridge was built at Poughkeepsie in 1889 by the Central New England Railway (CNE). The L&HR was then extended to Maybrook where the connection to the bridge was located. The dairy industry of Sussex and Warren Counties was a major customer and at one point generated 60% of the revenue. The L&HR also carried lime products from kilns at McAfee, produce from farms in the Great Meadows, and in wintertime, ice from the ponds of northwestern New Jersey.

In 1904, the New Haven Railroad (new owner of the CNE) closed down the car ferry across the river and directed all traffic through the newly enlarged yard at Maybrook. By 1912, this new gateway into New England had grown to become over three miles long and one of North America's largest rail classification yards.

At the turn of the century, the New Haven (known locally in some circles as "The Consolidated" because of the way it swallowed or *consolidated* foreign lines into the company.) was the villain of eastern American railroads. In 1904, the New Haven tried to acquire the L&HR. The L&HR's connections, the Erie, the DL&W, LV, and the Jersey Central were extremely alarmed at the prospect of the New Haven gaining a direct connection to the coal fields of eastern Pennsylvania. Together they purchased a controlling interest in one of the two companies that shared the ownership of the L&HR and stopped the incursion.

Traffic on the L&HR increased dramatically during World War I because the harbor in New York was very congested with tonnage destined for Europe. Troop trains bound for New England passed through this way. Later on during the thirties, when autos and trucks were becoming more prevalent, the passenger service was ended. An exception to this loss of passenger traffic was the semi-regular excursion trains run by the large connecting carriers that were the L&HR's biggest partners. The Jersey Central, the Lackawanna, and the Erie all ran these well-received special trains on this scenic route. Even during World War II, FDR's heavily guarded train from Washington was a regular sight, passing through on the way to Hyde Park, New York.

The railroad prospered until the 1960s when it became evident that the coal transporting business was being lost to fuel-oil and natural gas, alternatives that were better transported to New England by pipeline or barge. The loss of such a staple commodity was the death knell for much of the Northeast's rail network.

Bankruptcies ensued. The Penn-Central Railroad (PC) was created from the ghosts of the New York Central and the Pennsylvania railroads to stabilize the industry. An oil and water merger to begin with; PC was forced by the federal government as a condition of the merger to take in the New Haven and its high bridge at Poughkeepsie.

PC really did not want the bridge because all it connected with were the enemies of the PC. But the federal government, through the Interstate Commerce Commission, insisted that one train a day each way would be run by the PC to connect at the huge Maybrook yard. The PC grudgingly complied, but drastically down-sized the Maybrook yard in favor of the Selkirk (Albany) route into New England.

In the meantime PC entered bankruptcy in June 1970 and in 1972 the connecting dominoes fell also. LV, EL, Reading, and of course the L&HR all entered bankruptcy. Things staggered along until a suspicious fire on May 8, 1974, burned 700 feet of ties on the Pougkeepsie bridge (remember, the bridge PC never wanted). Very little in the way of structural components were damaged but PC refused to repair the bridge and it never saw another train again. (This 6,000 foot bridge today is under development as a pedestrian trail. Call 914-454-9649 for more information on their progress.)

After this, the L&HR only served local traffic in and around their home base of Warwick New York and things slowly shriveled up until they sold the property to Conrail in the mid 1980s. *The Lehigh & Hudson River Railway finally concluded its affairs in December of 1986 in NJ and in June 1987 in NY. Using the money from the sale to Conrail, it paid its bills and taxes and gave the remainder to its stockholders (about $65 a share), thereby preserving its record of never having lost their money, a feat of which very few railroads can boast.* (From the *L&HR Scenic Motor Tour* by the O&W Historical Society.)

Today the former L&HR is abandoned from Belvidere to Sparta Junction, while the northern section beyond Sparta has been rehabilitated by the New York, Susquehanna & Western Railroad and actually serves as their mainline. Although abandoned, much of the railroad's infrastructure remains intact, from its bridges, to its telegraph poles, milemarkers and signal posts.

Just over four miles of the L&HR rail bed are contained within the Pequest Fish and Wildlife Management Area, which runs roughly parallel with the Pequest River and U.S. Route 46. The trail is best suited for walking rather than biking or riding, and in some places minor detours must be made around fallen trees. Please note that this area is managed for hunting and fishing, so take appropriate precautions during the hunting seasons.

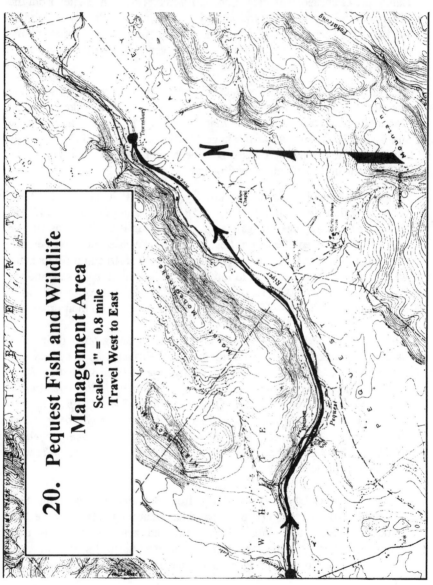

20. Pequest Fish and Wildlife Management Area

Scale: 1" = 0.8 mile

Travel West to East

0.0 miles: Starting at the trail-head in the town of Townsbury, and heading in a southwesterly direction.

0.2 miles: Inside a curving cut, on the right you'll see a cast concrete milepost which is typical of those found along the L&HR. The post states the mileage to the Maybrook, New York and Belvidere, New Jersey junctions. In this case Maybrook (MB) is 63 miles away, and Belvidere (BD) is 9 miles distant.

0.4 miles: An abandoned livestock underpass goes beneath the rail bed here, a reminder of the once robust dairy industry. The underpass provided livestock access to the river which otherwise would have been cut off by the railroad's construction in the early 1880s. This was a neighborly thing for the railroad to do.

1.3 miles: A steel bridge passes over the Pequest River. Route 46 parallels the trail for the next 1.5 miles.

2.6 miles: The rail bed passes behind some nearby houses, and at one point a minor detour must be made to get past some residential debris.

2.9 miles: Second bridge passes over the Pequest River.

3.0 miles: To the south, just up the hill area, you see the well-preserved remnants of an old iron furnace. Its foundations are still easily visible, and large piles of slag testify to its once productive past.

3.1 miles: Up the hill to the south is the old Delaware, Lackwanna & Western Railroad (DL&W) mainline, which parallels the L&HR for the next mile. Constructed in the 1860s, this was the DL&W's main line until 1911, when the Lackawanna Cutoff was opened north of here.

4.1 miles: A large concrete viaduct passes overhead which once carried the DL&W mainline over the Pequest River and the L&HR. A creamery and a small station were located here. This was on the map as Butzville. A junction was also made here for a small branch that led to an iron mine about two miles to the south. This point, near the intersections of Route 31 and Route 46, marks the end of state owned property and thus the end of the trail.

AMERICAN RAILROADS

IN PARTNERSHIP WITH ALL AMERICA

21 Sussex Branch Trail
Sussex Branch of the Lackawanna Railroad (DL&W)

Endpoints: Waterloo Road at Allumuchy State Park in Byram, to Decker Road in Lafayette.
Location: Sussex County, townships of Byram, Andover, Newton, Hampton, and Lafayette
Length: 14.8 miles
Surface: Cinder, gravel and original ballast
Map(s): Stanhope and Newton East in the U.S.G.S. 1:24,000 series, and Newark and Middletown in the 1:100,000 series
Uses: All non-motorized uses.

To get there: Take exit 25 off of I-80 to Route 206 north. In about 1.5 miles you will take a left onto County Route 604, also marked as Waterloo Road. This turn will be just after the Shell Gas Station. Follow this about 1.0 miles toward Allumuchy State Park and look for the relatively large parking lot on the right. It is directly opposite Continental Drive. There is plenty of room to maneuver Ford F-350s with horse trailers, though it is bumpy at times.

Contact: Kittatinny Valley State Park
P.O. Box 621, Andover, NJ 07821. 973-786-6445
For info in the city of Newton, call Vince Dominach 973-383-3521 ext. 226

Local Bed & Breakfasts:
Crossed Keys B&B, 289 Pequest Rd., Andover, NJ 07821. 973-786-6661
Whistling Swan B&B, 110 Main St., Stanhope, NJ 07874. 973-347-6369
Wooden Duck B&B, 140 Goodale Rd., Newton, NJ 07860 973-300-0395

Local resources for bike repair/rentals:
Andover Cycle Center, Route 206, Andover, NJ 07821. 973-786-6350.
(right on the trail at **5.1 miles**)
Coyote Bike'N Ski, 9 Main St., Sparta, NJ 07871. 973-729-8993

In 1848, Abram S. Hewit, the owner of an iron manufacturing business in Phillipsburg and Trenton, wanted to access the ore that was known to be in the Sussex County town of Andover. The major mine there was only 7 miles from the port of Waterloo on the Morris Canal, so he proposed to build a 40-inch narrow-gauge line that would be a mule drawn operation. It would transport the ore to the transfer docks in Waterloo and then barge the material to Phillipsburg on the Delaware River. It was known as the Sussex Mine Railroad and became operational in 1851.

In 1853, it was decided to change the route slightly and extend the line to Newton. The new track was built to standard gauge specifications and the company had a new name as well. "The Sussex Railroad." In 1864, a new owner by the name of John I. Blair took over and extended the line to Branchville with a spur line to the Iron Furnace at Franklin. (See Ride # 18, Paulinskill Valley Trail.)

As a local carrier, the Sussex Railroad became successful and attracted the attention of the major railroad in the area, the Delaware, Lackawanna, & Western Railroad (DL&W or Lackawanna). In 1881, the Lackawanna took over to prevent the Sussex from joining with another N-S road being built in New Jersey. (This future line would be known as the Lehigh & Hudson River Railroad, one of the numerous "anthracite roads" that rose to transport that hard coal from eastern PA into New England.) It then became the Sussex Branch of the Lackawanna and underwent a series of measures to upgrade and modernize. The traffic base on the line was also diversified beyond the ore business. Lackawanna was very actively marketing milk traffic to major cities so an agrarian branch like this was very heavily involved in that effort. In fact, the last dairy that was a regular shipper of milk was the Henry Becker & Son plant at Straders, a small community between Augusta and Lafayette. This creamery shut down in late 1964 and was said to be the last creamery in the state of New Jersey to ship by rail.

The Depression saw the first major track reduction at the spur from Branchville Junction to Franklin. The furnace there was no longer competitive with Midwestern plants and was closed down.

The merger between Erie and Lackawanna in 1960 (now known as Erie-Lackawanna-EL) created much duplicate trackage. Consequently, the management of the new company, which was dominated by Erie men, downgraded some of the Lackawanna lines, including the Sussex Branch. As a result, the level of through traffic business that connected at Andover Junction with the Lehigh and Hudson River Railroad saw a serious decline. Six short years later, in 1966, the tracks north of Andover Junction to Newton were pulled out and the line north of Sussex Junction in Stanhope saw fewer and fewer trains until the last one in 1969. The Sussex Branch was not part of the plan that created Conrail in 1976 so it stayed with the other unwanted and unprofitable routes of EL. The track languished in the weeds until 1977, when it was scrapped. In 1979, the southern section of right-of-way from Netong to Andover Junction was sold to the state of New Jersey Department of Environmental Protection (DEP). In 1982, the segment north of Andover Junction to Branchville was sold to the New Jersey DEP and the trail is now managed by the State Park Service within the Division of Parks and Forestry.

The historic area at the beginning of the trail contains the restored 19th century community of Waterloo Village. The Morris Canal was built to move some of the iron mined in the surrounding hills. The railroad was actually first built to transport iron to the canal port at Waterloo. Of course, the railroad eventually took over and grew in importance in the valley and eventually the canal was abandoned.

The parking area you are now in was actually part of a three-way junction with the prongs of the fork facing to the south. The straight track came in from Waterloo where the Lackawanna mainline passed by. The west leg came in from a stone quarry only a short distance away and the east leg went to Stanhope as part of a 1901 cutoff project built to shorten the distance to that community.

21. Sussex Branch Railroad Trail
Scale: 1" = 1.6 miles   Travel South to North
Mile 0.0 - 7.0

0.0 miles: Like many in New Jersey, this trail-head offers a portable toilet. The trail itself starts out in fine fashion, plenty wide and of good ground. Old ties are bulldozed to the side and a little original ballast is still here.

0.2 miles: Jefferson Lake is on the right. On the north end, there are signs that a siding diverged to the east. This is the Ice House siding. A common industry for railroads to serve prior to refrigeration was an ice harvesting company. They would set up on a fresh water lake that was close to a major population center, and cut and store ice for the long summer ahead. The railroad provided a customer for the ice, as well as a transportation mode. Today, a YMCA day camp is located on this site.

0.4 miles: Stream nearby leads to Cranberry Lake. In some areas, you will notice a meandering parallel railroad grade. This was the right-of-way for the Sussex Mine Railroad. Built in the early years of the 19th century to transport the iron ore to the canal, it was kept in operation until the newer steam railroad was completed. The Sussex Mine Railroad was not built according to the higher standards of the steam line, so it went around many of the hills that were cut through by the steam line. Look in this area for a cast iron marker on the right. You travel on a slight fill made of cinder.

0.7 miles: Benches for observing the waterfall cascading off the hillside to the right. This is near the former Cascade Mine.

1.0 miles: You are going upgrade. A 1-mile marker here is of modern construction and sports a hiker icon display. Concrete culvert; footings for a signal, probably one of the semaphore types that populated this line.

1.1 miles: 20- to 25-foot high arch bridge over the stream.

1.4 miles: A number of bluebird houses will be seen. These were built by a Byram Township Girl Scout troop, which volunteered to maintain the trail.

1.7 miles: Going by a set of guard rails that keeps cars off the trail. The South Shore Road is approaching and close by. This is an access road for lake dwellers. Some marshes appear as we get close to Cranberry Lake.

1.9 miles: Grade crossing of South Shore Road runs on the right.

2.0 miles: Parking lot for users of the small boat launching area.

2.1 miles: More guard rails to keep cars out of the trail., and a small parking lot. Cranberry Lake was a "destination" years ago. Much like the NYO&W's service to the Catskills; the Lackawanna ran a similar operation to this and other resorts near here. At Cranberry Lake, around the turn of the century, an elaborate resort development was constructed. (In the Lowenthal-Greenburg book, *The Lackawanna in Northwest New Jersey*, this period is described as the "Holiday Decade.") The Lackwanna provided the transport in and also coincidentally built the resort, a common practice among trolley companies. Cranberry Lake Resort had a sudden rise and an equally precipitous decline in only 10 years; by the time of the first World War it was but a memory. Today the former summer residences have been converted to year-round use.

2.3 miles: A park 'n' ride lot is accessible from Route 206. Trail-head parking is available at this site as well.

2.4 miles: Grade crossing of West Shore Road.

2.8 miles: A cut brings the paralleling Route 206 to a perspective above you. You are going slightly downhill here.

3.0 miles: Grade crossing of Whitehall Hill Road, where a divergence from the trail must be made. With modern highway reconstruction, the right-of-way of the rail-trail has been squeezed into a narrow cut that doesn't drain well. You should plan to stay on Whitehall Hill Road for a short distance to bypass this bad section. The speed limit for automobiles here is 25 mph and it is a bit of a narrow and winding road, so exercise caution.

3.4 miles: The trail is now apparent on the right and on a fill as the road jogs to the left. It is a little narrow in the beginning on the trail, again due to a small washout. Look on the left for the ruins of a small house with large trees growing within.

3.6 miles: The fill now has grown to be about 70 feet tall above Route 206 and about 40 feet above Whitehall Hill Road.

3.8 miles: You are now passing over "The Hole in the Wall." This arch bridge was installed in 1853 to allow Whitehall Hill Road to rejoin Route 206; typical Lackawanna ballast constructed of cinder. Look for the occasional ballast and ancient ties in the area also.

4.1 miles: Back onto level ground with some rocky out crossings on the right and the start of a slope up to the left.

4.3 miles: Footing for a signal tower; dimensions of approximately 12 x 12.

The Hole in the Wall

4.4 miles: Timber type bridge is seen following a "Bridge Out" sign. Deck girder bridge with timbers that are fairly rotted. Bridge is about 18 feet long and it crosses a wagon/farm underpass. It is easily crossed with care. However, it is officially closed.

4.6 miles: The trail passes under the Pequest Fill of the Lackawanna Cutoff via a concrete tunnel. The top of the structure lies about 40 feet overhead. A couple of telegraph poles remain. They are of the type that held over 26 insulators on each arm and some can still be found intact.

The immense structure that lies above you was one of the last big railroad projects built in the eastern United States. The Lackawanna Cutoff was built to by-pass a few tunnels in western New Jersey that were major headaches with their propensity for flooding. This route was shorter than the original by about eleven miles. But the noteworthy thing about the Cutoff was the size of the numbers throughout the project.

"To build the 28.45-mile Cutoff required 14,000,000 cubic yards of cuts and 15,000,000 cubic yards of fill. One fill, the Pequest Fill, across the valley south and west of Andover, took 6,250,000 cubic yards and, at 110 feet tall and three miles long, was the largest railroad fill ever built. Seventy-three bridges and viaducts were constructed, providing an opportunity to re-align several rural roads. At the western end of the Cutoff, two great concrete viaducts over the Paulins Kill and the Delaware River, gave the Lackawanna another chance to employ superlatives, for the Paulins Kill Viaduct, over 1,100 feet long with a maximum height of 115 feet, was then the largest concrete bridge in the world." (From *The Lackawanna Railroad in Northwest New Jersey*)

The last passenger train to run on that line was an AMTRAK inspection train in 1979. The next train was the scrap train that pulled out the track in 1985. Today, this line is in the news again as there is talk of re-opening it for commuter trains between Scranton, PA, and Hoboken, NJ.

4.7 miles: On the other side of the tunnel below Pequest Fill are some old houses as well as a small pond on the left. This is actually a man-made pond. When the huge fill was being constructed, the railroad bought sections of land along the right-of-way to use as "borrow pits," where material was scooped to build the towering fills. They dug so deep in these pits that they went below the water table, hence the large number of 'ponds' such as this one along the way. By the time you reach the third house along the right-of-way, the surrounding land is right at grade.

4.8 miles: Power substation on the left, then into the same level as Route 206, where there will be a grade crossing at High Street in Andover. The RoW is just adjacent to the highway now. Grade crossing of Maple Street. The Jersey Analytical Services building was once rail-served.

5.0 miles: Grade crossing into the town square area at County Road 517, where a signal relay box from the days of the Lackawanna presides over the intersection. Mounted between two 8 x 8 concrete posts, with a metal roof and wooden wainscoting sides, it marks the convergence between past and present. Railroad Avenue is the street on the left, lined with colonial and Victorian style houses.

5.1 miles: Grade crossing at Smith Street. The back side of the stores that front on Route 206 are visible here. Andover Cycle is located in this complex as well as some food and drink places. There are numerous antique stores out on Route 206 and the local historical society is nearby with an interesting photo display of the building of the Cutoff. Back on the trail and just in from Smith Street, the state has gated the RoW to keep out cars. It was in this area that the passenger depot for Andover was located.

6.3 miles: Route 206 has dropped away again and you are going downhill.

6.5 miles: Interesting stone culvert brings water away from the trail and to the highway on the right.

6.6 miles: The residential neighborhood seen here is rather interesting. One house has built a fence that borders the trail but they have also put in a gate so they can use the trail. In many cases across the country, where the neighbors have fought the construction of the trail, tall stockade fences are built. Then slowly over time, gates to the trail appear. Kind of interesting....

6.3 miles: Trail narrows considerably here as the growth of the brush has squeezed you onto a gentle slope leading to the Andover Diner. A fine place to eat any time.

6.4 miles: Concrete signal bases can be seen here, probably for the semaphore-type signals that used to be on this line. The system here protected the crossing at Andover Junction, where the Lehigh and Hudson River Railroad (L&HR) intersected the Lackawanna. The L&HR also maintained "their" Andover Station at this area. The trail will lead you to the right to Route 206. This is because the bridge ahead is out on the Sussex Trail. When on 206, take a left; shortly you'll be going over the grade crossing of the L&HR where the state has erected a sign noting "Abandoned Railroad Crossing." (They have left the rails in the road for some reason.) It should be noted that the right-of-way of the L&HR in this area is privately owned and not open to the public.

7.1 miles: An alternate parking area is located on the east side of Route 206. Look for the large sign marking the trail-head as *The Sussex Branch Trail*. Once again, a portable toilet is provided here for your convenience. Starting on the trail you'll notice that the surface is a little grass-covered on a cinder base.

7.4 miles: A causeway that divides two bodies of water. The larger one on your left is known as White Pond. Look for the swans and other water fowl.

7.6 miles: Into the woods again with another canopy of hardwood trees overhead. Look on the left for remains of a stone wall, a sign that this young forest was once a working farm. Large rocks are here in the form of a cut.

7.9 miles: A fill has appeared which takes you above the bog on the left. Grade crossing of road in this area will parallel you for a while.

8.1 miles A small stand of trees as well as a meadow owned by the state.

8.2 miles Grade crossing of the farm access. Look across the road and you'll see an unusual white-painted, wrought aluminum gate with ornate trim. This is an entry way to the Kittatinny Valley State Park.

8.5 miles: Now entering a small but rocky cut.

8.7 miles: Here is a big fill about 25 feet tall and straight as an arrow.

9.1 miles: Still on a bit of a fill as some power lines cross overhead. The forest is cut back where the power lines pass. Look for the large rocks here.

9.2 miles: On a fill about 40 feet tall; a modern industrial park on the left.

9.6 miles: Grade crossing at Yates Avenue where a Schwan's Ice Cream distributorship is located. No retail here, only wholesale. The street running parallel on the left is Stickles Pond Road, a residential neighborhood.

9.9 miles: A steep downgrade to the highway known as County Route 616-Newton-Sparta Road. A small unofficial parking area is across from Drake's Pond and the Al Lago Restaurant. When the railroad passed through, it did so by way of a bridge over the road. This was one of those low clearance bridges that was a hazard to traffic, so it was taken out. Cross over the highway to the east side and follow a short distance to where another trail-head parking area is located near a billboard announcing "Welcome to Newton." The trail continues behind this sign. Note: The trail for the next 1.0 mile is within the city limits of Newton where the right-of-way of the Rail-Trail is not really an open and maintained trail. Parts of this section are overgrown and parts have been encroached on. A detour routing onto the streets of Newton might be appropriate.

Contact Newton authorities for up to date info at 973-383-3521.

10.1 miles: Grade crossing at Hicks Avenue and Prospect Street. Keller Welding and Paint-Ball Supplies, an unlikely corporate combination, is located here. To stay on the streets of Newton, and avoid potential construction and Rail-Trail abutter problems, take a left here and then right onto Sparta Avenue - County Route 616. Follow this for about 0.3 mile and take right onto Diller Avenue. Take next left, onto Spring Street where you can rejoin the trail again at the 10.7 mile mark. All the interesting industries and buildings described here can be viewed from the streets.

10.2 miles: Rather overgrown and narrow; the surrounding ground drops away to bring you onto a fill about 25 feet high. More accurately, a larger and longer fill used to be here but it was taken out when the railroad was abandoned to provide some easier access to the other side. Be careful of the guy wire for the last pole as you descend the fill.

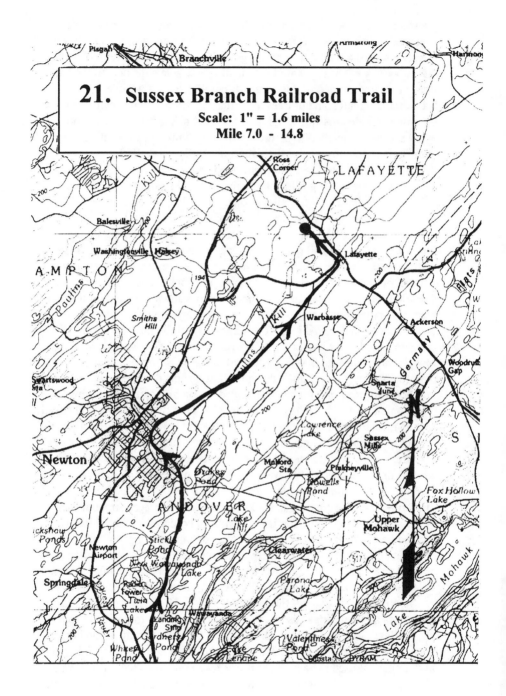

21. Sussex Branch Railroad Trail
Scale: 1" = 1.6 miles
Mile 7.0 - 14.8

10.4 miles: Off the fill and down to the bottom at ground level and soon you'll be in the back of the Karen Anne Quinlan Center of Hope Hospice.

10.5 miles: Into the parking lot for the condo complex that was once the H.R. Merriam Shoe Factory. This large mill is a great example of what can be done with obsolete factories. Go to the front side of the site to see the ancillary businesses, such as the pub, that is a natural fit within the whole complex. At the north end of this section are a few other industries, the first being a metal sheathed structure that was a part of the Sussex Dye and Print Works, a receiver of ink. Across the right-of-way is the Texaco Oil Depot where tank cars of lubricants used to be received.

10.7 miles: The concrete wall on the left is about 0.2 mile long and denoted the boundary of Railroad Avenue on the west side. The Hart & Iliff Lumber Company was on the east side of this area. Part of this complex burned down in 1951. The remaining sections were still in business until the late 1980s. The office part is now the home of the local Moose Club. The beautifully restored building on the west side of the yard as you approach Spring Street was the DL&W Freight Depot.

10.8 miles: Grade crossing at Spring Street. This is where the passenger station stood. The railroad used to have a switch right at the north side of Spring Street to bring cars up the steep grade and into a fuel oil complex owned by the Hart & Iliff Company. The stone house at Spring Street has been featured in many archive photos from the steam era.

10.9 miles: Into a small cut; steep upgrade to the right. Look for the Lackawanna era concrete fence posts nearby. Hart & Iliff Fuel Oil Dealer on the left. Just beyond, on the east side, is another rail-served industrial complex. Probably a rail-to-truck terminal, it seems to be vacant today. The parallel running street on the east is Stuart Street.

11.0 miles: Grade crossing of Trinity Street. The initial area past the street is a little rocky; it seems to be part of a storm drain run-off site. More concrete type fence posts here. This is part of a line of such posts that were spanned by barbed wire. Thomas Edison had a concrete plant in nearby New Village; he manufactured concrete houses here. Through his affiliation with the Lackawanna Railroad, he was able to get contracts for vandal-proof posts. In fact, the Lackawanna Railroad built many of its structures out of concrete, including the immense viaducts on the Lackawanna Cutoff.

Each cut and fill 'Cross dale and hill
Has made The Shortest shorter still.
I now delight like arrows flight
To speed o'er Road of Anthracite.

Verse from a Lackawanna Railroad advertisement
published shortly after the Cutoff was finished

11.1 miles: Out of the built-up part of Newton now and into a marsh area that is part of the watershed for the Paulins Kill. Some spectacular water fowl are visible here, so be on the lookout for them and for the 3-foot diameter cast-iron culvert.

11.4 miles: Slight fill here; you are still in the wetlands.

11.5 miles: Moor's Creek crossing. This site has the remains of a bent timber trestle which reportedly was the only wooden bridge on the Lackawanna Railroad. (Remember the propensity for using concrete.) Unfortunately, this means there is no longer a bridge here at all, but the stream is not much more than possibly a damp shoe. At only 8 feet wide and 10 inches deep with a gravel bottom, it is a small challenge to cross.

11.6 miles: 18-inch metal culvert is seen as you get into another hardwood forest and out of the marshes. The unnamed pond on left will likely have many swans and possibly some Canada Geese, who winter in this area.

12.0 miles: This area was known as Branchville Junction where a line called the Franklin Branch came in from the east. Wooden boxes on the ground are battery boxes which powered the semaphore signals that protected the junction. Also here are the footings for a water tank built in 1905, along the mainline in the middle of a wye-track configuration.

12.1 miles: A station was built here in 1905 but burned in 1911. The concrete platform curbing is still visible. This area, though only about 0.2 miles from the NYS&W crossing at Warbasse, had no direct connection with that railroad. Passengers who wanted to go to destinations served by the NYS&W had to guess when the next train would be coming through.

12.3 miles: Grade crossing of County Route 663 and then immediately after is Warbasse Junction. The Lackawanna called this area NYS&W Crossing, while the NYS&W named it Warbasse Junction after the family that owned the land at one time. Note the small marker at the crossing. To go straight ahead will bring you to a bridge out over the small stream. The best route is to take a left at Warbasse Junction, travel on the Paulins Kill Valley Trail (NYS&W) a short distance to the trail-head parking lot, take a right onto County Route 663 and go across the bridge over the stream. The trail will start again on the right as soon as you cross the stream. Where the trail-head parking lot sits is the site of a creamery which had a siding in the early years of this century.

13.0 miles: Grade crossing of Route 94 -- a busy highway, so please be careful. Lafayette Village, a retail shop complex, is just across the adjacent highway bridge over the Paulins Kill.

13.3 miles: Into the lightly forested woods now with the river running parallel. Look for the beehives in the woods, maintained by a bee-keeper who accesses them by way of a pressure-treated walk-bridge to his property.

13.5 miles: An example of recycling old rail-served industry, the complex found here is still in some sort of modern use. A three-car siding is evident with stone foundation and stucco-finished surface. Rail dock is pre-stressed concrete. This area also had the small passenger shed that served as the station in the last years of passenger service.

13.6 miles: The Rail-Trail is gated to stop cars from entering at the grade crossing of Morris Farm Road. Then you come into an area of antique shops that occupy converted buildings. The one on the Rail-Trail is the Lafayette Mill Antique Center. It was a granary complex at one time and had rail-served doors. Spaced at the 40-foot intervals that were the normal length for boxcars of the era, it is a typical re-use of a rail-served industry. The doors have been converted to walk-in doors for retail traffic.

13.7 miles: On a fill now that is shelf down to the right. The park, with tennis courts and man-made lake, is a fine place to relax on a summer day. (Courts are open to residents only, however.) A little further up is a wetlands with more interesting wildlife. Man-made dam here allows water to get to the lower area.

14.0 miles: You will encounter a wet trail in this short area. Try the left side; it is the best side through the cut that is about 25 feet high.

14.2 miles: Grade crossing of small country road. Also found here is a relay cabinet with the battery boxes nearby. Edison Wet-Cell Batteries were the batteries of choice and were re-filled with acid on a regular basis by signal maintenance crews, who sometimes threw the bottles into the woods when the section boss wasn't looking. Consequently, if you rummage around any area that had battery boxes, you might find a bottle or two that has been lying in the weeds for 50+ years.

14.4 miles: Single cross-arm telegraph pole, along with some farm fields, providing a worthwhile camera vista.

14.5 miles: BRIDGE OUT sign here. Take the right path down to Decker Road below. Deck girder bridge used to be on this site, but only the concrete abutments and wing walls remain today. Go up onto the trail again.

14.8 miles: Unusual barbed wire fence in this area is done with railroad ties. A few telegraph poles remain in place, but the bridge over the Paulins Kill is gone. This is what is meant by "A Bridge Too Far." The end of the trail. In the future, the trail will continue about 6 miles further. At the time of this writing there are 5 missing bridges in this short distance. The State of New Jersey intends to restore the bridges for trail users in the near future (possibly as early as the end of 1998) so check with the folks at Kittatinny Valley State Park, 973-786-6445, to see if work has been completed when you visit the trail.

The Tunkhannock Viaduct, the largest concrete bridge in the world at 2,375 feet long. Located 20 miles west of Scranton, Pennsylvania, it still sees regular rail traffic today.

ERIE LACKAWANNA RAILWAY COMPANY

DINING SERVICE

Dinner Menu

"Erie Lackawanna spectacular Tunkhannock Viaduct at Nicholson, Penna. — One of the railroad engineering wonders of the world."

The Friendly Service Route

22 Traction Line Recreation Trail

Morris County Traction Line

Endpoints: Route 510 and Morris Avenue in Morristown, to Convent Station in Madison
Location: Morris County, Morristown and Madison
Length: 2 miles with 1 mile extension scheduled to open in 1998.
Surface: Asphalt
Map(s): Morristown, U.S.G.S. 1:24,000 series
Uses: Non-motorized uses, except horses.

To get there: Take I-287 to Morristown and then take Exit 36. Go east on County Route 510 approximately one block to the intersection with Morris Avenue. Park on this street where approved. This is near the site of George Washington's Headquarters.

Contact:
Morris County Park Commission
P.O. Box 1295, Morristown, NJ 07962-1295   973-326-7600

Local Lodging:
Westin-Morristown Hotel, 2 Whipanny Rd. Morristown, NJ 07960
973-539-7300
Madison Hotel, 1 Convent Road, Morristown, NJ 07960
973-285-1800

Local resources for bike repair/rentals:
Marty's Reliable Cycle of Morristown, 173 Speedwell Avenue
Morristown NJ 07960   201-538-7773.

Part of the following information is from a brochure published by the New Jersey RailTrails, a state-wide non-profit group that works to turn abandoned railroads into multi-use public trails. Information about joining can be obtained by writing to P.O. Box 23, Pluckemin, NJ 07978, or by calling 215-340-9974.

Located within the cosmopolitan and historic community of Morristown, Morristown National Historic Park is located at 10 Washington Place and can be reached via Route 124.

The park commemorates the two winter encampments of General George Washington and the Continental Army during the Revolutionary War. It is divided into units encompassing 1,700 acres. The first unit, located directly across from the beginning of the Traction Line Trail, consists of Washington's Headquarters, which houses a museum and extensive Revolutionary War library, and Ford Mansion. Other units include Fort Nonsense, Jockey Hollow Encampment, and the Wick House.

Other historical attractions include: the Morris Museum with its collection of fine arts, anthropology, geology, decorative arts, history, and natural science; The Schuyler-Hamilton House, the colonial home of Dr. Jabez Campfield, a Revolutionary War doctor; the Museum of Early Trades and Crafts in Madison, with hands-on activities for young visitors pertaining to life in the 18th and 19th century; and the Macculloch Hall Historical Museum and Gardens, a brick federal style mansion. For information on these sites and others in the area, visit the Historic Morris Visitors Center, 14 Elm Street, Morristown, NJ 07906 or call 973-993-1194.

The Traction Line Recreation Trail, located between Morris Avenue in Morristown and Convent Road in Madison, was previously part of a 2.6-mile segment of the Morris Traction Company Trolley Line (MTC). The MTC, which was chartered in 1899, operated 32 interconnected routes from Lake Hopatcong to Elizabeth. This segment was opposed by wealthy land owners, and subsequently was denied a franchise to operate on public roads. Because a trolley company lacked the land condemnation authority possessed by railroads, MTC incorporated itself in April of 1913 as a steam railroad, Morris Railroad, and thus obtained the needed property. Trolley service between Morristown and Maplewood began in February of 1914. When it was no longer able to compete with the automobile, MTC was sold at public auction in October of 1927. The new owners then sold the property and franchises to the Public Service Company and, in March of 1928, the New Jersey Public Utilities Commission approved the dissolution of the corporation, ending MTC's brief history.

The Traction Line Recreation Trail was developed by the Morris County Park Commission through a federal grant and was dedicated in June of 1986. The land was donated by Jersey Central Power and Light Company (JCP&L). A chain link fence separates the trail from the NJ Transit passenger trains. Thus, this corridor is also famous as being one of the country's original "rail-with-trail" corridors. There are now over 50 similar trails in operation across the country.

Completion of a one-mile extension beyond Convent Road and Danforth Road in Madison was dedicated on June 16, 1998. Land for the extension was donated by JCP&L and Fairleigh Dickenson University.

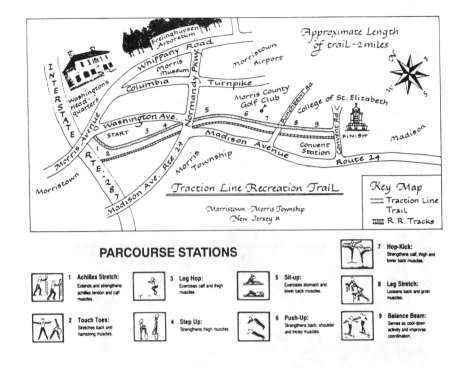

PARCOURSE STATIONS

1 Achilles Stretch: Extends and strengthens achilles tendon and calf muscles.

2 Touch Toes: Stretches back and hamstring muscles.

3 Log Hop: Exercises calf and thigh muscles.

4 Step Up: Strengthens thigh muscles.

5 Sit-up: Exercises stomach and lower back muscles.

6 Push-Up: Strengthens back, shoulder and tricep muscles.

7 Hop-Kick: Strengthens calf, thigh and lower back muscles.

8 Leg Stretch: Loosens back and groin muscles.

9 Balance Beam: Serves as cool-down activity and improves coordination.

0.0 miles: The trail starts out by going downhill in a short steep section. There is a marker nearby describing Washington's Headquarters Museum, which sits across the street. Parking is also available there or on the streets.

0.1 miles: Here is a parking area for the Jacob Ford Apartment complex that is adjacent to the trail in this area. The first of the nine Par Course Stations is here also. "Fitness for everybody," the sign says.

0.3 miles: Another apartment complex is on the left and the New Jersey Transit high-speed electrified commuter line is on the right and separated from trail users by a chain-link fence. Par Course Station # 2 is located here and an uphill grade begins.

0.4 miles: There are houses on the left with a garden on the embankment that leads down to the houses.

0.5 miles: The third Par Course Station, the "log hop" is here. The grade uphill has ended and the trail still abuts the NJ Transit commuter line and its protective fence.

0.8 miles: Par Course Station #4 is here. This is the "Step Up." Also, users pass under the Normandy Street bridge.

0.9 miles: Par Course Station # 5 is here. Sit ups.

1.1 miles: Par Course Station #6: Push-ups are the activity here. Grade crossing of Kahn Road. New Jersey Transit has a signal tower with searchlight signals at mile marker 484.

1.5 miles: Grade crossing for a residential driveway. Par Station # 7 is here as well as the Morris County Golf Course and an office complex.

1.6 miles: Going over an old-fashioned cast concrete bridge which dates from the trolley days and spans Punchbowl Road.

1.7 miles: Par Station #8, the leg stretch.

2.0 miles: Par Station # 9, the balance beam. The Convent Station New Jersey Transit Station and the College of St. Elizabeth are here.

The Traction Line Recreational Trail passes under Normandy Street

23 West Essex Trail

Caldwell Branch of the Erie Railroad

Endpoints: Francisco Avenue (near the Great Notch railroad station) in Little Falls, to Arnold Way in Verona
Location: Passaic County, town of Little Falls, and Essex County, towns of Cedar Grove and Verona
Length: 3.3 miles
Surface: Cinder and gravel
Map(s): Orange, U.S.G.S. 1:24,000 series
Uses: All non-motorized uses.

To get there: The best place to park is at Community Park. Travel north on Route 23 (Pompton Avenue) 2.0 miles from Bloomfield Avenue, Verona, or south 2.3 miles from the Passaic River Bridge just south of Willowbrook Mall in Wayne. From either direction, turn east on Little Falls Road, Cedar Grove. Take Little Falls Road 0.5 miles to the Cedar Grove Community Park on the right. Park and go up the hill to reach the trail.

Contact:
Essex County Department of Parks, 115 Clifton Avenue,
Newark, NJ 07104. 973-268-3500

Local Lodging:
Prime Hospitality, 700 Route 46 East, Fairfield, NJ 07007. 973-882-1010

Local resources for bike repair/rentals:
Bike Land Inc., 461 Bloomfield Ave., Caldwell NJ 07006. 973-403-3330

Part of the following information is from a brochure published by the New Jersey RailTrails, a state-wide non-profit group that works to turn abandoned railroads into multi-use public trails. Information about NJRT can be obtained by writing to P.O. Box 23, Pluckemin, NJ 07978, or by calling 215-340-9974.

The West Essex Trail (WET) is located on the original grade of the Caldwell Branch of the Erie Railroad. The trail runs along cuts and fills through moderately hilly terrain past suburban houses and occasional wooded parcels. It is suitable for hiking, horses and off-road bicycles. It is not improved but has a good cinder base, with some sections covered with small gravel.

The WET is a low-key route through a suburban area. It passes through Cedar Grove Community Park, and features a high trestle over Peckman River, where the stream drops through a small gorge over exposed ledges of Watchung Basalt, the geologic basis of the First Orange Mountain. South of the present terminus is the only obvious railroad structure, the old Verona Freight station at Personnette Avenue, now a warehouse for Keifer Brush Company. Further on are the tunnel under Bloomfield Avenue, which is scheduled to be filled-in; the Grover Cleveland homestead, a state park near the trail in Caldwell; the Kiwannis Oval Park; and the Grover Cleveland Park, originally planned to be the southern terminus of the WET.

The Caldwell Branch was built between 1890 and 1892 as part of a real estate venture. The New York Suburban Land Company and the First Presbyterian Church of Caldwell chartered and funded the Caldwell Railway Company to accelerate the development and marketing of their extensive land holdings in Caldwell and what is now Essex Fells. The railroad failed and was taken over in 1893 by the Greenwood Lake Railroad, which built the original line through the Great Notch.

In 1898, the Erie Railroad took over the Greenwood Lake and from then on provided service on the Caldwell Branch. In 1904, the Morristown & Essex (M&E) established a connection at Essex Fells. The branch provided frequent passenger service to Jersey City, with service to Morristown over the M&E for a brief period. Usage peaked in the early 1920s. The stations along the line were: Cedar Grove, Verona, Caldwell, and Essex Fells, with a flag stop at Overbrook Hospital. (A flag-stop station was one that had a flag for passengers to display to the approaching train. Thus alerted, the engineer would stop and take on those passengers. Normally there would not be a stop.) The automobile caused a gradual decline in passenger traffic, and service to Morristown ended in 1928. All commuter service ended in 1966, and freight service ended in 1976 with the creation of Conrail.

The mileage guide is based at the northern end at Francisco Avenue. So, travel the slightly more than one mile to the end and then reset your odometer.

0.0 miles: Northern end of the trail at the active New Jersey Transit rail line. Do not walk along the railroad.
0.2 miles: Effective start at Francisco Road, with some parking on the streets to the west.
1.0 miles: Lenape Trail enters from the east and heads another 1.1 miles to the west. Going east, the Lenape Trail follows greenway, parklands, and some sidewalk stretches 14 miles to Military Park in downtown Newark, and is marked with yellow blazes. It temporarily ends at Little Falls Road to the west, but will eventually be extended.

1.1 miles: Grade crossing of Bowden Road.

1.3 miles: Community Park, which is where you started because it provides the best parking access. Also here is the Peckman River Trestle, which is sometimes closed. If it is, head down the grassy slope and through the trees, to the steel bridge over the river. Head back up the opposite side into the garden apartment complex, staying to the left of the buildings, on township land at the edge of the grass. Continue up the hill and turn right on the trail.

1.4 miles: Peckman River Trestle.

1.6 miles: Cross over Route 23 (Pompton Avenue).

2.0 miles: Essex County Hospital Center grounds on the left and right sides.

2.2 miles: Bridge over Hospital Center access road.

2.6 miles: Cross Durrell Street.

2.9 miles: Cross Fairview Avenue where some street-side parking is available.

3.3 miles: This is the effective end of the trail at Arnold Way. Do not park on or leave by way of this street as it is a sensitive area where people are uneasy about trail-users using the limited parking resources.

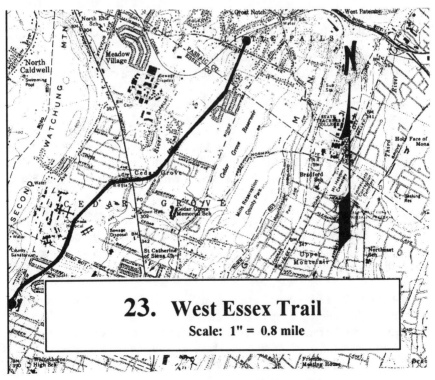

23. West Essex Trail
Scale: 1" = 0.8 mile

24 Woodbine Railroad Trail

Cape May Branch of the Pennsylvania Railroad (before the PRSL merger)

Endpoints: Fidler Hill Rd. to Grant Ave. within the borough of Woodbine
Location: Cape May County, borough of Woodbine
Length: 1.4 miles
Surface: Gravel and dirt
Map(s): Woodbine, U.S.G.S. 1:24,000 series
Uses: All non-motorized uses.

To get there: Take the Garden State Parkway to Exit 20 to U.S. Route 9 south to County Route 550 north. As soon as you get near Woodbine itself, a railroad bridge is overhead. Take the first left after the overpass onto Fidler Hill Road. At the first right (Dehirsch Avenue), park where it is safe and allowed. The trail starts here and heads north alongside Route 550.

Contact:
Susan Peck Land Use Administrator, Borough of Woodbine
809 Franklin Street, Woodbine, NJ 08270. 609-861-5301

Local Bed & Breakfast:
Henry Ludlam Inn, 1336 Route 47, Woodbine NJ 08270 609-861-5847

Local resources for bike repair/rentals:
Delsea Bike Shop, 116 Route 47 North, Cape May Courthouse, NJ 08210
609-465-9420
Hale Sports, 5 Mechanic St., Cape May Courthouse, NJ 08210.
609-465-3126

Once the Pennsylvania and Reading lines in the area merged in 1933, this line was among the first to be abandoned with the end coming in 1936. This line was the ex-Pennsy line to Cape May which ran from Manamuskin to Cape May and was 36 miles long.

Coming this far down to South Jersey means you might want to take in the nearby Cape May. This is the oldest resort community in the country. Cape May has the largest intact collection of Victorian housing in the country, with over 600 examples.

0.4 miles: The Woodbine Developmental Hospital is on the left. This is a large multi-building complex that is a state-run facility and used to be a customer of the railroad, receiving cars of coal for the power plant. Note the interesting stand of white pine trees between you and the Hospital.
0.5 miles: This large open area between Dehirsch Avenue and Route 550 is actually the railroad corridor.

0.8 miles: Grade crossing at Heilprin Avenue. You are coming into an area of residential housing and this is the end of the white pine trees. There is a large town common with some recently planted trees on the edges. The icon of Woodbine will be visible now; the Woodbine water tower.

1.0 miles: Grade crossing of Madison Avenue, then Jefferson Avenue where a pizza shop can be found. The Woodbine Fire Department can be found at the Adams Street area.

1.2 miles: Grade crossing at Washington Street-County Route 557. This is the major intersection in town. Lincoln Avenue is just ahead and this area used to have a second set of tracks that diverged away from the main track. It is unclear where this siding went, but most likely it was to a small industry that is now long gone.

1.4 miles: The in-town section of the trail ends at Grant Avenue. The RoW goes into the woods here and is basically clear though not officially open as a trail. The nearby Belleplain State Forest has some rail-trail corridor (about 7 miles) in their jurisdiction that is a continuation of this RoW. Some of the trails within the forest are also open to ATVs. There are also many other trails at Belleplain State Forest. To get there, follow Route 550 northwest out of Woodbine to the village of Belleplain, and then look for signs leading to the state forest.

24. Woodbine Railroad Trail
Scale: 1" = 0.4 mile
Travel Southeast to Northwest

177

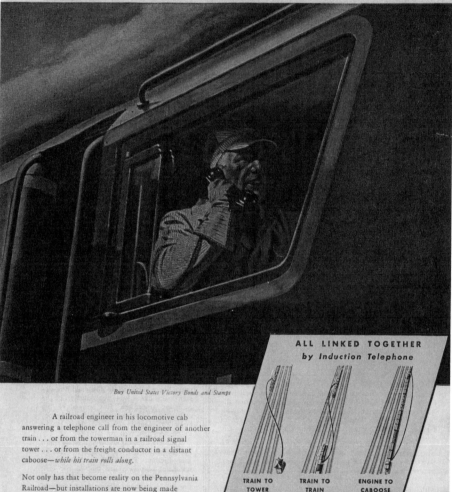

Taking a Phone Call
AS HE ROLLS ALONG!

Buy United States Victory Bonds and Stamps

ALL LINKED TOGETHER
by Induction Telephone

| TRAIN TO TOWER | TRAIN TO TRAIN | ENGINE TO CABOOSE |

A railroad engineer in his locomotive cab answering a telephone call from the engineer of another train . . . or from the towerman in a railroad signal tower . . . or from the freight conductor in a distant caboose—*while his train rolls along.*

Not only has that become reality on the Pennsylvania Railroad—but installations are now being made on the main line on a big scale.

This train telephone system is a creation of Pennsylvania Railroad research, worked out in conjunction with the Union Switch and Signal Company. Tested and proved, it adds still further to established signaling, communicating and safety devices which make American railroads the safest transportation in the world!

PENNSYLVANIA RAILROAD
Serving the Nation

Appendix:

Glossary of Terms

Railroad Bridge Architecture

Railroad Name Abbreviations

Resources for Maps

Books for Further Reading

Railroad Historical Societies

Hiking Resources

Equestrian Resources

Bicycling Resources

Glossary of Terms

BALLAST: Rocks, usually about 2-3 inches in diameter, placed below the ties and track area to facilitate drainage of water away from the track and also to prevent the growth of weeds.

CINDER: The refuse of burnt coal. This was used in the construction of some fills and sometimes was used as ballast or road construction.

CUT: An excavation in the ground to maintain the gentle slope required of a railroad.

FILL: An area raised to be above the surrounding ground to maintain the gentle grade. The material used in a fill is usually from a nearby cut.

GRADE: A term used to describe the degree of change from level. Railroads were usually not able to climb grades steeper than 5%; i.e., a five-foot rise for every one hundred feet of travel. It is rare to see any gradient steeper than 2.5% on an old railroad line listed in this book.

GRADE CROSSING: This is where a road crossed the tracks at the same level. Busier crossings usually had the protection of gates which lowered to block the automobiles. Some areas warranted a grade crossing watch-man who came out to manually put down the gate and prevent the cars from crossing, but this type of arrangement was usually not seen after the 1950s.

ROAD(S): Short for railroad, for example the Lackawanna road.

RoW: Right-of-Way is the route of the railroad and or trail.

TIES: Wooden timbers usually 8.5-feet-long, used to support and maintain the gauge of the rails.

1940s advertisement, courtesy of TRAINS magazine (Author's collection)

Basic Overview of
Railroad Bridge Architecture
Common to New Jersey

There are two basic categories that apply here.

1. **Deck Type** structures which have the supporting members underneath the bridge.

2. **Through Type** structures have the supporting members bestride or over the track.

These categories are further broken down by the following widespread construction materials.

1. **Girder** (steel). Usually made up of separate sections riveted with plates and angles to make for a strong but generally short bridge.

2. **Beam** (wood). Early bridges were commonly constructed of wood timbers.

3. **Truss** (wood or steel). A series of structural shapes fashioned into an open system that are generally variations of the letter "W." Wooden versions of this were often covered to prevent exposure to the elements, hence "covered bridges."

Other Variations of Bridges
and their Definitions

Trestle: A series of short bridges that are individually supported along the length. (Some books about rail-trails describe all railroad era bridges as "trestles").

Viaduct: Generally a stone structure that spans a wide valley.

Culvert: A pipe or box that is back-filled with dirt and gravel and used for drainage under a railroad.

Railroad Name Abbreviations

B & A; Boston & Albany Railroad

CNE; Central of New England

CNJ; Central Railroad of New Jersey

CR; Conrail

EL; Erie-Lackawanna Railroad

ER; Erie Railroad

DLW; Delaware, Lackawanna & Western Railroad (Lackawanna)

L&HR; Lehigh & Hudson River Railway

L&NE; Lehigh & New England Railroad

LV; Lehigh Valley

NH or NY, NH&H; The New York, New Haven and Hartford Railroad.

NYC; New York Central Railroad

NY&NE; New York & New England Railroad

NYS&W; New York Susquehanna & Western

O&W; New York, Ontario & Western Railway

Pennsy; Pennsylvania Railroad

PRSL; Pennsylvania-Reading Seashore Lines

PC; Penn-Central

RDG; Reading Railroad

RVRR, Rockaway Valley Railroad

Maps and Atlases

Available road maps and atlases of New Jersey are too numerous to make a complete listing here. However, bookshops or outfitters will have an abundant supply of local publications to help you find your way to the trails mentioned in this book. It is a good idea to obtain the appropriate map or atlas for the trail area you expect to visit. (Spend your valuable free time on the trail, not on the road trying to find it.)

The USGS topographic maps (known as "topos" or "quads") are useful for exploring these trails in the field. The relevant U.S.G.S. map names are mentioned in each trail's heading. Consult the yellow pages under "Maps -- Dealers" to obtain these useful publications. They cost about $6.00 each. With the Information Age upon us, perhaps the best way to obtain maps is to get the topographic map program from: MAPTECH Inc., 655 Portsmouth Avenue, Greenland, NH 03840. (800) 627-7236. They are makers of a user-friendly Windows-based CD-ROM which contains complete state coverage of Topo maps of major states, including one for New Jersey. MAPTECH maps were used to produce the trail maps in this book. The program retails for about $100.00. Their web site is *www.maptech.com*. Another source is Somerset Geographics, 4 East St., Doylestown PA 18901   215-340-9974

A good source for highway and street maps of New Jersey is:
Hagstrom Map Company Inc., 46-35 54th Road, Maspeth, NY 11378
800-432-6277

Lehigh & Hudson River Railway map from around 1920 (Author's collection)

For Further Reading
A guide to learning more about special places in New Jersey

Cawley, James and Margaret. *Exploring the Little Rivers of New Jersey*
Rutgers University Press, New Brunswick, NJ; revised by Little Rivers Club
in 1993.

Lowenthal, Larry. *The Iron Mine Railroads of Northern New Jersey*.
Dover, N.J.: Tri-State Railway Historical Society, 1981.

Lowenthal, Larry. and Greenburg, William T Jr.
The Lackawanna Railroad in Northwest New Jersey. Morristown NJ.

Archer, Robert F. *Lehigh Valley Railroad*.
Forest Park, Ill.: Heimburger House Publishing Co., 1977.

Lehigh Valley Chapter of the NRHS. *Railroads in the Lehigh River Valley*.
Allentown, PA.

Geist, Helen Hagerty, *The Califon Story*, Califon Historical Society

Snell, James P., *History of Hunterdon and Somerset Counties 1881*
New Jersey Historic Sites Inventory

Mastich, James et al. *Images of America: Lambertville and New Hope*,
Arcadia Publishing, Dover, NH. 1996

McKelvey, William J., Jr.
The Delaware & Raritan Canal: A Pictorial History, York, PA 1975

Gladulich, Richard M., *By Rail to the Boardwalk*
Trans Anglo-Books, Inc. P.O. Box 6444, Glendale, CA 91205

Stroup, John P., *Pennsylvania-Reading Seashore Lines*
Morning Sun Books, Inc. 11 Sussex Court Edison, NJ 08820 1996

David Trumbull-Marshall
Boyhood Days of Old Metuchen (reprinted 1979, Quinn & Boden for the
Metuchen Historical Society)

Lee, Harold., *A History of Ocean City*.
Ocean City, NJ. Friends of the Ocean City History Museum, 1995

Taber, Thomas T. III.
The Rock-a-Bye Baby, A History of the Rockaway Valley Railroad
Muncy, PA., 1972.

Paulinskill Valley Trail Committee.
The Paulinskill Valley Trail, Before and After. Hackettstown, N.J. 1996

O&W Historical Society. *Scenic Motor Tour of the L&NE.*
Middletown, NY. 1987

Krist, Ed and Krause, John. *The Lehigh & Hudson River*
(two volumes) Carstens Publications, Newton, NJ.

Krist, Ed and Krause, John. *Susquehanna.* Newton, NJ. 1980

Lee, Warren F. *Down Along the Old Bel-Del.* Albuquerque, NM

O&W Railway Historical Society. *Scenic Motor Tour of the L&HR.*
Middletown, NY: O&W Railway Historical Society, 1987

Olsen, Judith M. *Pemberton Township: A History*
The Friends of the Pemberton Community Library, 1976.

Nielsen, Waldo.
Right-of-Way: A Guide to Abandoned Railroads in the United States,
Maverick Publications (1992), P.O. Box 5007, Bend OR 97708.

Nehrich, John. *Milk Train Data Pack*
Published by the Rensselaer Model Railroad (1993),
Rensselaer Student Union, Troy, NY 12180-3590.

Shaughnessy, Jim. *Delaware & Hudson*
Howell-North Books (1967), 1150 Parker Street, Berkeley, CA 94710.

Walker, Mike. *Railroad Atlas of North America* Steam Powered Publishing
(1993), ISBN# 1-874745-00-5. You can order this for about $23.00 through
Carstens Publishing Co., P.O. Box 700, Newton, NJ 07860 (973-383-3355).
The atlas shows stations, junctions, yards, and tunnels. Original owning
company and current owners' names are also displayed.

Railroad Historical Societies

Camden & Amboy Railroad *Historical Society*
P.O. Box 3277, South Amboy, NJ 08879.

Conrail
Conrail Historical Society, Inc., P. O. Box 38, Walnutport, PA 18088-0038.

Central of New Jersey, Delaware, Lackawanna & Western, Lehigh & Hudson River, Lehigh & New England, Lehigh Valley, and Reading Railroads
Anthracite Railroads Historical Society, P.O. Box 519, Lansdale, PA 19446-0519.

Delaware & Hudson Railway *Bridge Line Historical Society*
P.O. Box 7242, Capital Station, Albany, NY 12224

Erie Lackawanna *Historical Society*
116 Ketcham Rd., Hackettstown, NJ 07840.

Lehigh Valley Railroad *Historical Society*
P. O. Box RR, Manchester, NY 14504-0200.

Middletown & New Jersey Railway *Historical Society*
325 Collabar Rd., Montgomery, NY 12549

N.J. Midland Railroad *Historical Society*
P. O. Box 6125, Parsippany, NJ 07054.

New York Central System *Historical Society*
P.O. Box 81184, Cleveland, OH 44181-0184

New York Susquehanna & Western Railroad *Historical Society*
P.O. Box 121, Rochelle Park, NJ 07662.

Pennsylvania Railroad *Technical & Historical Society*
Box 389, Upper Darby, PA 19082.

Pennsylvania-Reading Seashore Lines *Historical Society,*
P.O. Box 1214, Bellmawr, NJ 08099.

National Railway Historical Society
P.O. Box 58547, Philadelphia, PA 19102-8547.

The Railroad Enthusiasts Inc.
  3 Durham Lane., Gonic, NH 03839.

Railroad Station Historical Society, Inc.
  430 Ivy Ave., Crete, NE 68333.

Railway & Locomotive Historical Society
  P. O. Box 215, East Irvine, CA 92650-0215.

West Jersey Chapter, National Railway Historical Society
  P.O. Box 647, Palmyra, NJ 08065

*Extremely rare mile marker denoting kilometers as a primary distance.
Installed by the old New Haven Railroad around 1900*

Antique railroad crossing sign. Tens of thousands of these were once installed throughout the country; today, they are an expensive novelty item.

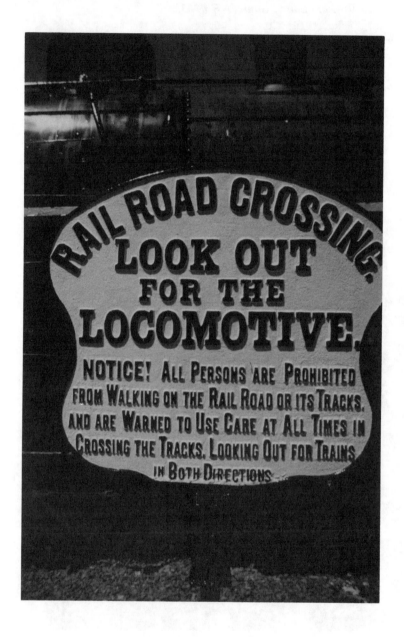

Hiking and General Trail Resources
in New Jersey

Appalachian Mountain Club (AMC)
    New York-North Jersey Chapter
        5 Tudor City Place, New York NY 10017
        212-986-1430 or -1431   http://www.amc-ny.org/
    Delaware Valley Chapter
        1180 Greenleaf Dr., Bethlehem PA 18017
        610-694-8677   http://www.enter.net/~dvamc

Canal Society of New Jersey
        P.O. Box 737, Morristown, NJ 07963
        908-722-9556

National Park Service-Rivers, Trails, Conservation Assistance Program
        143 South 3rd St. Philadelphia, PA 19106
        215-597-6483

NY / NJ Trail Conference
        232 Madison Avenue, #802
        New York, NY 10016
        212-685-9699

New Jersey RailTrails
        P.O. Box 23
        Pluckemin, NJ 07978
        215-340-9974

New Jersey Trails Coordinator
        NJ Dept. of Environmental Protection
        CN404, Trenton, NJ 08625-0404
        609-984-1173

Paulinskill Valley Trail Committee
        P.O. Box 7076,
        Hackettstown, NJ 07840
        908-852-0597

Equestrian Resources
in New Jersey

New Jersey has a special affinity for the horse. In fact, the horse is the state animal.

The New Jersey Horse Council was established in 1970 to serve the interests of the New Jersey Horse Industry. There are more than 60,000 horses in the state making New Jersey the most densely populated state with horses in the nation. The industry is worth over $4 billion and generates $600 million annually. (Statistics from a brochure by the New Jersey Horse Council)

One of the best resources about matters equestrian is a magazine called *All about Horses; the Complete Directory for the New Jersey Equine Industry.* Published by the Hudson Reporter, P.O. Box 3069, 1400 Washington Street, Hoboken, NJ 07030. 201-798-7800. This a must-have for all equestrians in New Jersey.

Central Jersey Horseman's Assoc.

886 Bowman Road
Jackson, NJ 09527

Central Jersey Trail Riders

P.O. Box 53
New Gretna, NJ 08224

Delaware Valley Horseman's Assoc.

P.O. Box 345
Ringoes, NJ 08551

Hidden Valley Riding Club

1235 Rt. 9 South
Cape May Courthouse, NJ 08210

New Jersey Trail Ride Association
P.O Box 578
Chatsworth, NJ 08019
609-894-1659

Hunterdon County Horse & Pony Association
3 Lynwood Drive, Lebanon, NJ 08833

New Jersey Horse Council
25 Beth Drive
Moorestown, NJ 08057-3021
609-231-0771
njhorse@aol.com
http://silo.com/equine/horse.htm

Somerset County Horse & Pony Club
Ms. Susan Data-Samtak
P.O. Box 84, Pluckemin, NJ 07978
e-mail: Pasovasz@aol.com

Susan Data-Samtak of the NJRT and her Paso Fino breed horse,
enjoying the Ogden Mine Trail (Photo by John Samtak)

Bicycling Resources
in New Jersey

Bicycle Advocate, NJ DOT
P.O. Box 600, Trenton, NJ 08625. 609-530-8062

Bicycle Touring Club of No. Jersey
Matt Kuruc, P.O. Box 839
Mahwah, NJ, 07470
973-284-0404
http://home.att.net/~btcnj

Central Jersey Bicycle Club
732-225-HUBS

International Mountain Bicycling Association
P.O. Box 7578
Boulder, CO 80306
303-545-9011

Jersey Shore Touring Society
732-747-8206

League of American Bicyclists
202-822-1333

NJ Cycling Conservation Club
732-972-8822

Princeton Free Wheelers
P.O. Box 1204, Princeton, NJ 08542
609-882-4739

Shore Cycle Club
609-625-0249

South Jersey Wheelmen
609-848-6123

County Locator Maps

County	Ride #
Atlantic	12
Burlington	19
Cape May	15, 24
Essex	23
Gloucester	14
Hunterdon	4, 5, 6
Mercer	6
Middlesex	13
Monmouth	7, 8, 10
Morris	1, 2, 3, 5, 16, 17, 22
Somerset	6, 11
Sussex	9, 16, 18, 21
Warren	18, 20

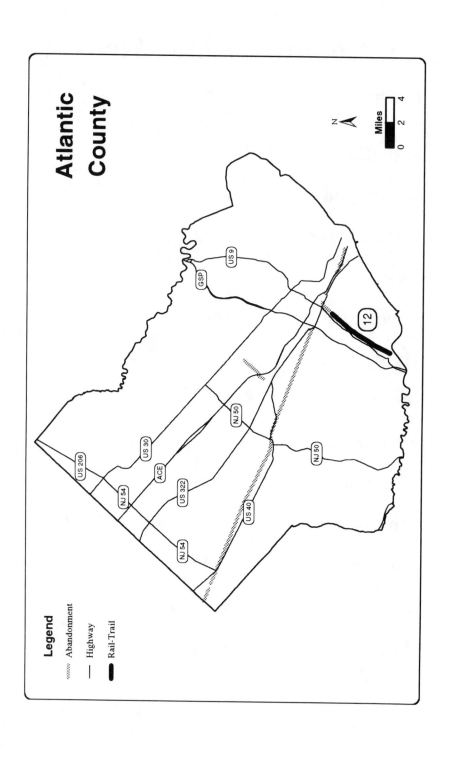

Atlantic County

Legend

- Abandonment
- Highway
- Rail-Trail

US 206

NJ 54

NJ 54

US 30

ACE

US 322

US 40

NJ 50

NJ 50

GSP

US 9

12

N

Miles

0   2   4

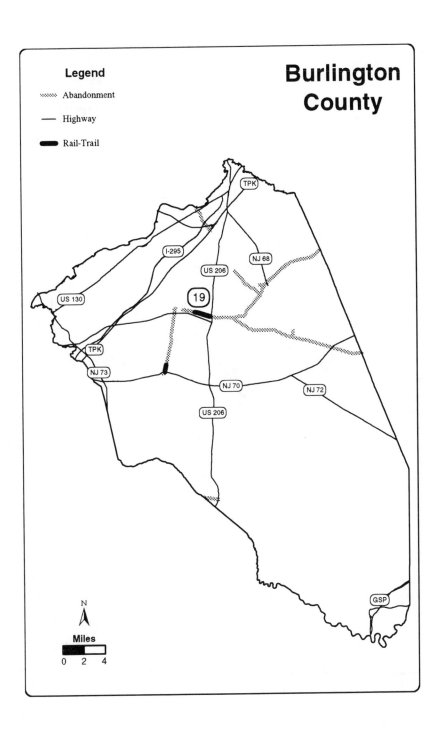

Legend

~~~~~ Abandonment

—— Highway

▬▬ Rail-Trail

Burlington County

TPK

I-295

NJ 68

US 206

US 130

19

TPK

NJ 73

NJ 70

NJ 72

US 206

GSP

N

Miles

0 2 4

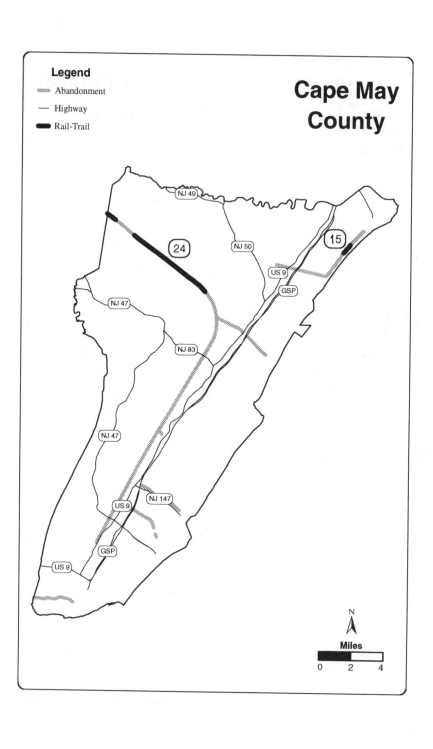

Legend
- Abandonment
- Highway
- Rail-Trail

Cape May County

NJ 49

24

NJ 50

15

US 9

GSP

NJ 47

NJ 83

NJ 47

NJ 147

US 9

GSP

US 9

N

Miles
0   2   4

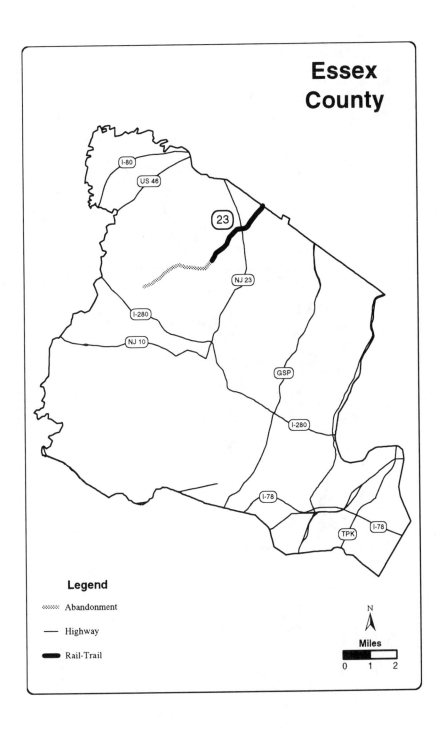

Essex County

Legend

~~~~~~ Abandonment

——— Highway

▬▬▬ Rail-Trail

N

Miles

0   1   2

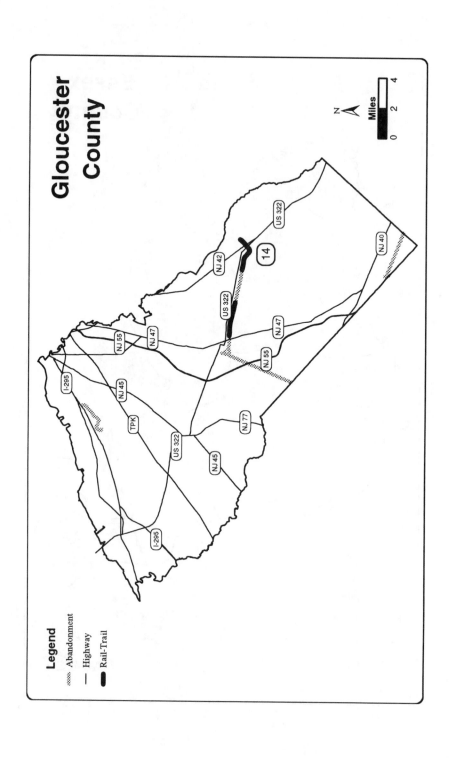

Gloucester County

Legend

Abandonment
— Highway
Rail-Trail

N

Miles
0   2   4

US 322
NJ 42
14
US 322
NJ 47
NJ 55
NJ 47
NJ 40
NJ 55
I-295
NJ 45
TPK
US 322
NJ 45
NJ 77
I-295

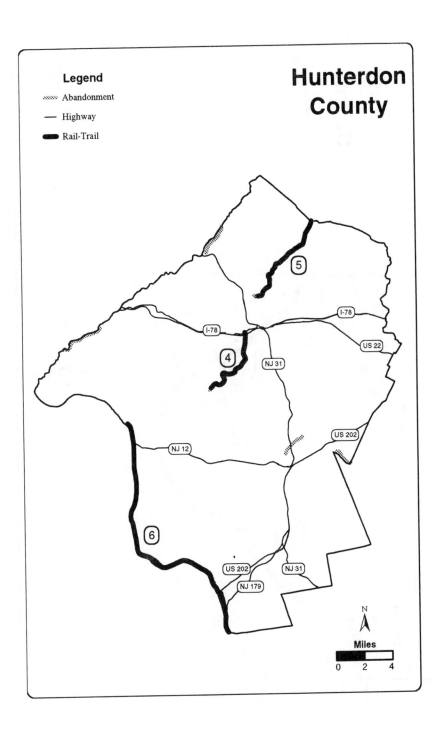

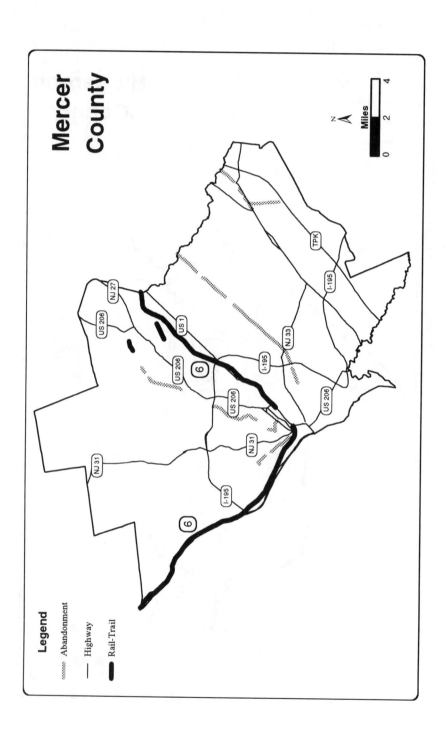

Mercer
County

Legend

Abandonment
Highway
Rail-Trail

Miles

0   2   4

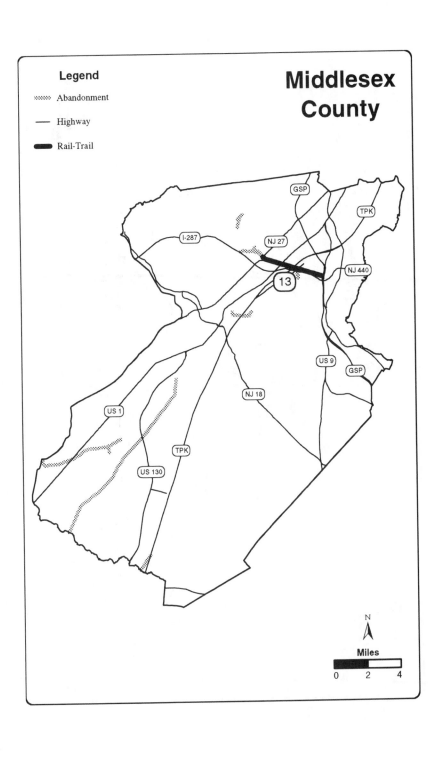

Legend

- Abandonment
- Highway
- Rail-Trail

Middlesex County

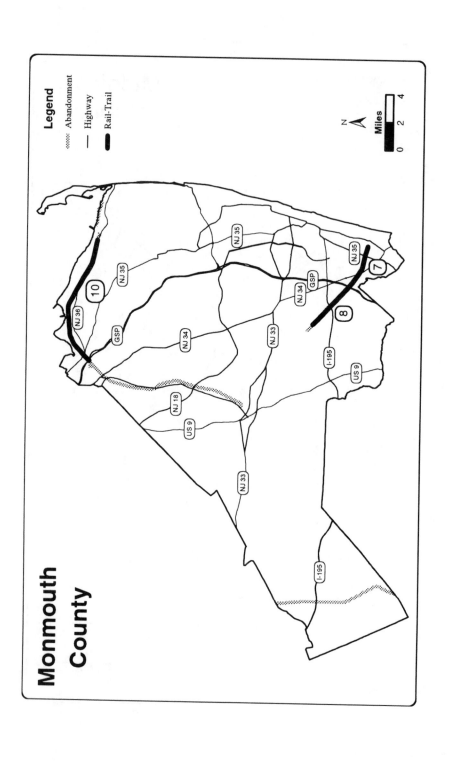

Monmouth County

Legend

- Abandonment
- Highway
- Rail-Trail

N

Miles
0 2 4

10

NJ 36

NJ 35

GSP

NJ 34

NJ 18

US 9

NJ 33

NJ 35

NJ 33

I-195

NJ 34

GSP

8

US 9

I-195

7

NJ 35

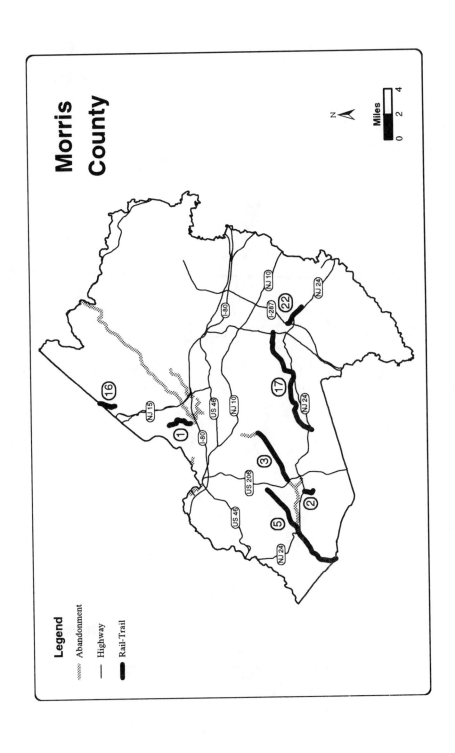

Morris
County

Legend

~~~~~ Abandonment

— Highway

▬ Rail-Trail

N

Miles
0 2 4

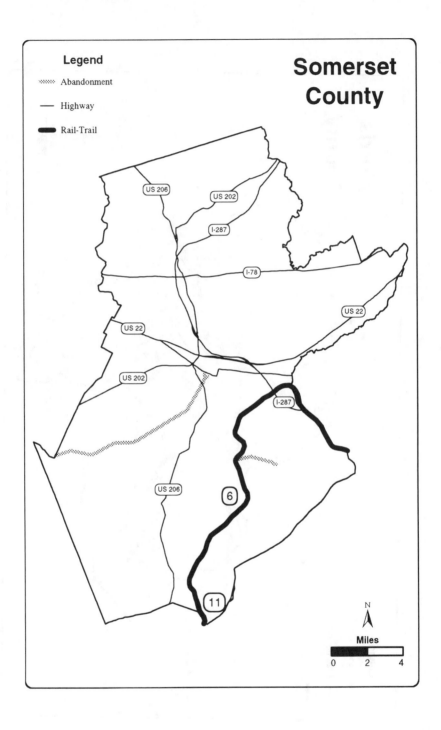

Legend

~~~~~ Abandonment

—— Highway

▬▬ Rail-Trail

Somerset County

US 206

US 202

I-287

I-78

US 22

US 22

US 202

I-287

US 206

6

11

N

Miles

0   2   4

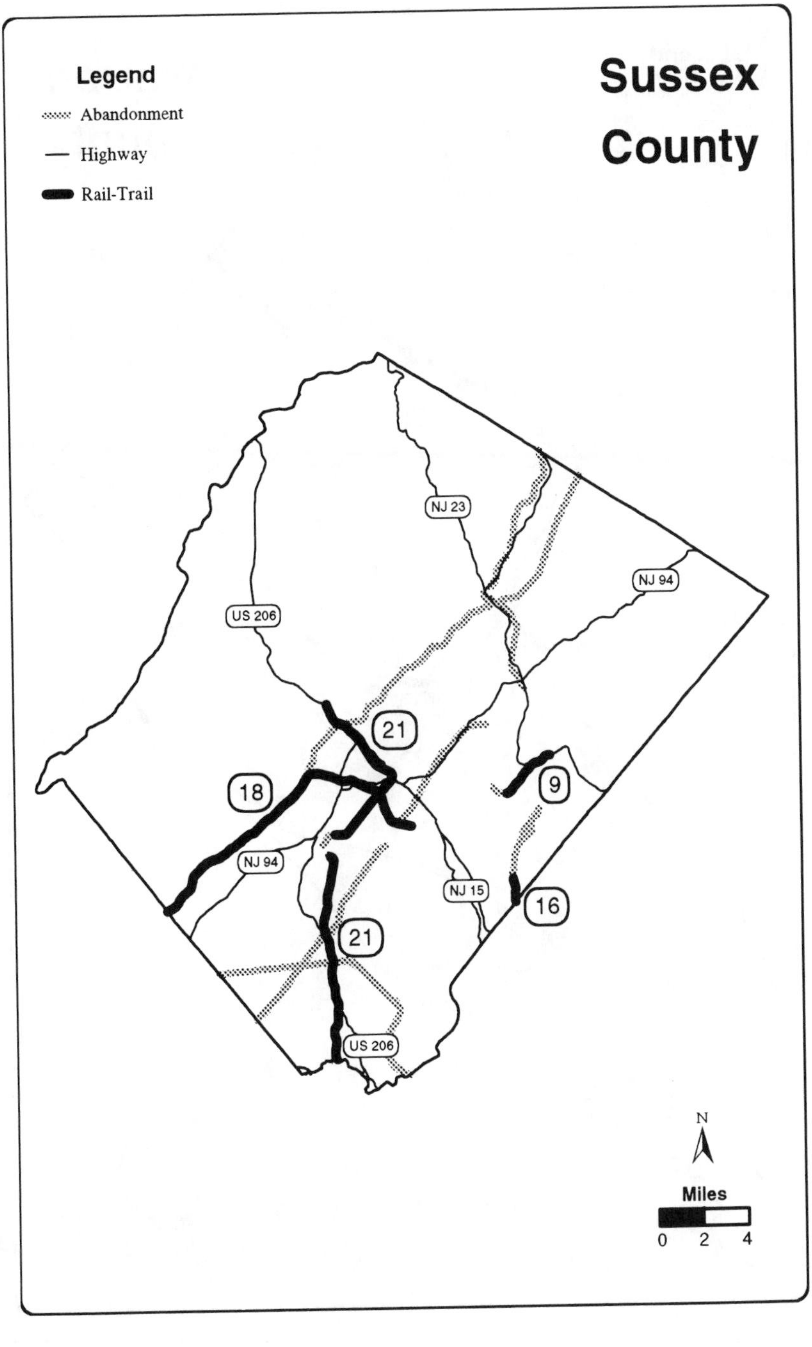

Legend

~~~~~ Abandonment

— Highway

■■■■ Rail-Trail

Sussex County

NJ 23

NJ 94

US 206

21

18

9

NJ 94

NJ 15

16

21

US 206

N

Miles
0   2   4

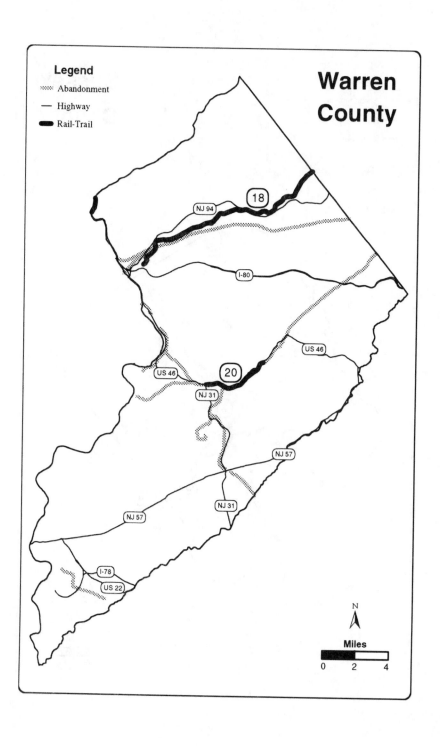

Legend

Abandonment

Highway

Rail-Trail

Warren County

18

NJ 94

I-80

US 46

US 46

20

NJ 31

NJ 57

NJ 31

NJ 57

I-78

US 22

N

Miles

0   2   4

Notes

Notes

New England Cartographics
Price List

Maps

Holyoke Range State Park (Eastern Section)	$3.50	_____
Holyoke Range/Skinner State Park (Western)	$3.50	_____
Mt. Greylock Reservation Trail Map	$3.50	_____
Mt. Toby Reservation Trail Map	$3.50	_____
Mt. Tom Reservation Trail Map	$3.50	_____
Mt. Wachusett and Leominster State Forest Trail Map	$3.50	_____
Western Massachusetts Trail Map Pack (all 6 above)	$13.95	_____
Quabbin Reservation Guide	$3.95	_____
Quabbin Reservation Guide (waterproof version)	$5.95	_____
New England Trails (general locator map)	$2.00	_____
Grand Monadnock Trail Map	$3.50	_____
Connecticut River Map (in Massachusetts)	$5.95	_____

Books

Guide to the Metacomet-Monadnock Trail	$8.95	_____
Hiking the Pioneer Valley	$10.95	_____
Skiing the Pioneer Valley	$10.95	_____
Bicycling the Pioneer Valley	$10.95	_____
Hiking the Monadnock Region	$10.95	_____
High Peaks of the Northeast	$12.95	_____
Great Rail Trails of the Northeast	$14.95	_____
Golfing in New England	$16.95	_____
24 Great Rail Trails in New Jersey	$16.95	_____

Subtotal Order _____

Please include postage/handling:

$0.75 for the first single map and $0.25 for each additional map;
$1.00 for the Western Mass. Map Pack;
$2.00 for the first book and $1.00 for each additional book.

Postage/Handling _____

Total Enclosed _____

Order Form

To order, call or write:
New England Cartographics
P.O. Box 9369, North Amherst MA 01059
(413) - 549-4124
FAX orders: (413) - 549-3621
Toll-Free (888) 995-6277

Circle one: *Mastercard* *Visa* *Amex* *Check*

Card Number____
Expiration Date ____________________________________
Signature____
Telephone (optional) ________________________________

Please send my order to:

Name ____
Address ____
____
Town/City _______________________________________
State ______________________ **Zip** __________________